SOLO
LAWYER
BY DESIGN

A PLAN FOR SUCCESS
IN ANY PRACTICE

GARY P. BAUER

Cover design by Tamara Kowalski/ABA Design

Printed in the United States of America.

21   20   19   18   17   5   4   3   2   1

Library of Congress Cataloging-in-Publication Data

Names: Bauer, Gary P. | American Bar Association. Solo, Small Firm and
   General Practice Division, sponsoring body.
Title: Solo lawyer by design / Gary P. Bauer.
Description: Chicago, Ill. : American Bar Association, 2017. | Includes
   index.
Identifiers: LCCN 2017008506 (print) | LCCN 2017012277 (ebook) | ISBN
   9781634258012 (ebook) | ISBN 9781634258005 (softcover : alk. paper)
Subjects: LCSH: Solo law practice—United States.
Classification: LCC KF300.5 (ebook) | LCC KF300.5 .B38 2017 (print) | DDC
   340.068—dc23
LC record available at https://lccn.loc.gov/2017008506

Discounts are available for books ordered in bulk. Special consideration is given to state Bars, CLE programs, and other Bar-related organizations. Inquire at Book Publishing, ABA Publishing, American Bar Association, 321 N. Clark Street, Chicago, Illinois 60654-7598.

www.shopABA.org

Contents

Part II   Get on Track to Start Your Own Practice

Part III   Marketing: Your Biggest Challenge, Your Greatest Opportunity

Part IV   Miscellaneous Good-to-Know Stuff

Part V   Client Control Issues

Part I

Finding Your Passion in the Practice of Law

Chapter 1

Why This Book? Some Preliminary Matters

For nearly twenty years, I have been actively involved in helping students better understand the business of law and how they might use their law degrees to their greatest advantage. Often I have found that greater preparation for law practice as a "solo" practitioner is the best answer for many of them. For others, I have developed materials and other tools to help them become more successful whether as solos or working for others in a shared office environment or law firm setting. The business of law, as distinguished from legal theory and practice, begins with a realistic understanding of market forces and the practical limitations but also the opportunities for law school graduates.

Too many commentators predict doom and gloom for the legal profession. I believe, after you read this book, you will see opportunities that others fail to see. In addition, it provides a prescription to address the problems you may encounter as well as a method of fostering the greatest return for your efforts. To some degree, preparing you for the world of practice that you will encounter today is not enough. What I hope to do is to prepare you for the world of practice for the future as well. Whether you go solo or work for someone else, you will find the planning process I recommend to be a valuable tool for your advancement. But, you will need to follow through to prepare a plan and execute on your plan.

A Little History

Before law schools were creating "incubators," advertising "practice ready" graduates, and offering classes to train soon-to-be lawyers about the business of law, Western Michigan University (WMU) Cooley Law School had already started programs that focused on practical legal scholarship. We had already identified the need to help our students better understand the opportunities that solo practice had to offer.

GPSolo Concentration Formed

In 1999, WMU Cooley Law School established a concentration to support students who wished to go solo. As appointed chair of the GPSolo and Small Firm Concentration, I was committed to supporting those students and finding ways to help them establish their way to success in solo practice. At first, I worked through our Career and Professional Development Center. We offered books that provided business startup guidance for those students. Among many of the books in that library was *How to Start and Build a Law Practice* by Jay Foonberg.

In the course of my tenure as chair of that concentration, I frequently interviewed solo practitioners in the field. Many solo practitioners, whom I subsequently interviewed, said that the Foonberg book was their bible. They said that they felt the concepts that Foonberg laid out were valid, practical, and useful in their practices. *How to Start and Build a Law Practice* was, and still is, valuable for someone interested in going solo. I have tried not to replicate the material Foonberg covers in his book in this text. Also, as his frame of reference Foonberg uses attorneys who have left law firms where they have been practicing with a book of clients and significant savings to fund their startup. This book goes beyond the approach in Foonberg's book to give you information tailored for law students who are considering a practice of their own. It will provide a road map on how to go about preparing for solo practice *right out of law school*. It can be done, and many of my students have gone solo, right out of law school and have been very successful.

All students who chose to declare the GPSolo and Small Firm Concentration were required to enroll in certain electives designed to prepare them for the types of cases that most solo practitioners tend to find as their area of practice. For instance, these included family law, bankruptcy, estate planning, as well as mortgages and land contracts. They had some flexibility in scheduling with "recommended" and "highly recommended" elective options with greater emphasis on those areas of the law that were more popular among solo practitioners listed in the latter category. In addition, they were required to enroll in a practicum, a practical experience in the law school (internship) or outside the law school (externship) as a requirement for graduation.

As the GPSolo Concentration evolved under my leadership, I felt that we were still missing an important element in counseling students. I found myself counseling more and more students to go into the field where they intended to practice to explore realistic options for their specific practice setting. Eventually, I developed and offered a directed study that was structured in a manner that helped them develop a business plan that made sense for their unique circumstances. At the same time, I invited experienced and new solo practitioners to the law school to tell the students about their unique experiences as solo practitioners. After their presentations, the students would question them on the realities of practice; the good, the bad, and the ugly of solo practice.

Survey Solo Practitioners in Michigan

In an effort to find out what my students needed to know to succeed, in 2003, I circulated a five-page survey with almost 100 questions to about 2,800 solo practitioners in the state of Michigan, and received 339 completed surveys. More detail on the results of that survey follow below.

Creation of the Solo by Design Listserv

The next step was to establish a Google Group for students who wished to go solo, or recent grads who established solo practices right out of law school. In it, I provided guidance and resources for them as well as a forum for them to post questions or comments to one another as they wished. The listserv became, and continues to serve for them as a forum to communicate with one another—to provide resources, referrals, and answers for their peers. Prior to publication of this book, that group had grown to more than 300 subscribers.

Courses Specifically Geared to the Business of Law

At WMU Cooley, we also created several other courses for students that were designed to provide them with a better understanding of how they might be attuned to the business of law. They include Accounting for Lawyers,

Entrepreneurship for Lawyers, Transition to Legal Practice, and, of course, Law Practice Management (which uses the Foonberg book as its text). In January 2015, I started a blog, sololawyerbydesign.com which, you guessed it, offers information for all attorneys about the practice of law. Some of that material is included in this book as well—but not all of it. I invite you to visit my blog for updates and even more information which is designed to help you succeed in practice.

Chair State Bar of Michigan Law Practice Management and Legal Administrators Section

In an effort to be better informed about the issues that confront law firm practice, I became involved in the Law Practice Management Section of the Michigan State Bar and eventually became the chair of that organization. In that role, I was directly involved in the creation of the Michigan Institute of Continuing Legal Education (ICLE) with Shel Stark, the program director for ICLE. That program has become an annual event with a strong following and repeat attendance year after year. I have served on numerous committees for the American Bar Association (ABA) and State Bar of Michigan, all of which focused on the changing nature of practice and how the regulation and education of the newest members of the Bar will need to adapt to those changes to remain relevant. My input is sought because of my extensive experience in this area of practice support.

Author *Solo Lawyer by Design*, the Book

Everyone who knows me knows that I have been committed to helping my students and graduates succeed in the business of law. This book is the culmination of my efforts and a ready reference for you to tap into my extensive experience. I sincerely believe that this book will become a resource that you will revisit as your business matures. Finally, I have decided to write this book to enable you to better understand what you will face as you explore establishing yourself as a solo practitioner. My aim is to have you better informed so that you fully appreciate the opportunities and obstacles that you will face as you consider this path as your professional practice platform. This book is not designed to sell you on solo practice. In fact, if you decide solo practice is not for you, I am fine with that. If you find that you do not have the personal characteristics to weather the storm of inclement legal pressures, then I have moved you toward success as much as if I have helped you decide that you are cut out for solo practice.

This is a book written to help prelaws, law students, and recent graduates, as well as seasoned practitioners understand where they best fit into the legal practice environment. I hope to give you the tools to help you weather the rapidly changing marketing developments which present new and difficult obstacles to successful practice. But where technology taketh away, it also opens doors to new opportunities to expand your area of influence in new and efficient ways. Throughout this book, I have incorporated a number of true stories to help demonstrate certain concepts and hopefully to be somewhat entertaining.

Chapter 2

Why Should You Listen to Me?

I have been on a mission to help students find success as solo practitioners long before it became popular to do so in the law schools. Since 1999, when I was designated as chair of the GPSolo Concentration at my law school, I set out on a mission to find ways to enhance the prospects of entrepreneurs in ways that others are just now beginning to explore. In 2003, I prepared a five-page-long questionnaire and surveyed nearly half of all the solo practitioners in the state of Michigan. I did this to determine what it took to be successful in practice as a solo practitioner and gathered data to help me pursue my goal of designing a program for my students that would be of value to them. I sent out several thousand of those lengthy surveys and 339 completed questionnaires were returned. This was an amazing rate of return considering the length and complexity of the questionnaire. Interestingly, the responses did not provide what I was seeking—the key to success as a solo based on traits that students exhibited while law students like their GPA, student debt load, military service, gender, or other factors. Instead, the most telling part of the survey was the "Comments" section in which respondents were able to comment on the question: "Please write any advice that you have for students considering going into solo practice on the back of this page." And they did, almost everyone had handwritten comments. Some of them wrote extensive comments. The questionnaire was anonymous, but the respondents could self-identify if they wished.

Some of the comments were expressions of frustration with their decision to go solo. Many of them recommended working in a law firm before striking out on their own. Keep in mind that survey was done in 2003. Since then, technology has radically transformed the practice of law and communication light years away from the technology that was in use even then. Many of those comments recommended having a law library of hardcover volumes and being dependent on yellow pages and expensive phone systems to operate a law practice. Many of those norms no longer apply. What I do throughout this book is to take you on a journey to find what you need to know today and for the future. Much of the advice in the survey comments still holds true today; some of it must be tempered with changes in technology and legal platforms that are available today.

In 1999 when I was appointed chair of the GPSolo Concentration, I focused on the style of practice management that the students would be engaged in, and less on the substantive law that they practiced. I could see back then that many of our graduates ended up going solo not by design but by accident. Many of them sought employment in law firms. When they were not successful finding the job they wanted, they ultimately hung out their shingle. So I read everything I could concerning establishing a solo practice in books, on the Internet, and through interviews with other solo practitioners.

Through the years I have gathered a tremendous amount of resource material and counseled many students who have expressed a desire to go solo. I have also counseled many students who did not know what they wanted to do upon graduation. Helping them approach their decision with information that was beneficial to them and would help them establish a sound business plan was my first priority. I have counseled hundreds of students and kept in touch with many of them through emails, phone calls, and in person. Almost daily, I have students seek my advice on how they might succeed in establishing themselves in business after graduation. On many occasions I have invited solo practitioners and others to come in and speak to my students about the good, the bad, and the ugly of going solo.

Today there is a trend among many law schools to do some of what I've been doing for years. Many law schools offer "incubators," which are courses to help recent grads establish their own legal practices. Also, there are many commercial resources available online, both free and fee based. This book is an attempt to help you better understand how to work through all of the material that is available and decide which approach is best for you considering your interests, your strengths, and your weaknesses. As I tell my students I am not trying to create mini-mes. Rather I help them find their way in their environment, with their personal skills and deficits. This must be a path that will be tailored to their unique needs and positive attributes.

There is no single formula that works for everyone. I find many of the students trying to emulate what others are doing and replicate what they are doing. That is a mistake. You need to look at what other lawyers are doing, and in most cases, don't do that.

I also come from a marketing background and think and process information in ways that many of my colleagues do not. I don't necessarily know all the answers. However, many of my students who have gone out on their own are doing very well financially. That's not to say they're getting rich. However, I believe that they are better able to achieve balance in their lives and find financial security. They do this in an environment and under terms that they find are coincident with their values and sustained happiness. I see far too many lawyers who are unhappy in this profession. No one told them or showed them how to create a plan and structure their practice so that they could be happy practicing law.

My sincere hope is that after reading this book you will have found the formula for happiness in your life while practicing law. I hope you come to an understanding of whether or not solo practice is for you. Or should you consider working for someone else because you do not have the characteristics to be able to be successful in solo practice? In fact, you may find upon reading this book, that the path you take will not be legal practice at all. Instead you may find, if you are entrepreneurial, that you create a different business model outside of the legal practice arena.

I hear many say that there are too many lawyers graduating from law school. They excoriate the law schools for graduating so many lawyers and cite that as the reason why so many lawyers are having a difficult time succeeding in practice. The problem isn't that we have too many lawyers. The problem is that too many attorneys practicing law do not understand how to sell their services effectively or they are misfits in the area of law that they practice. They never found their passion in the law.

I spent six years in sales and learned a great deal about how to communicate effectively with potential customers and close the deal. The last class of my estate planning course is a conversation with all the attending students about the fact that they will not be immediately recognized as valuable commodities upon graduation unless they take steps to make their value appreciated. The law school where I have taught is not ranked in the U.S. World News as a top tier law school. Yet I have successfully mentored hundreds of students through the process of entering the practice in a manner that helped them achieve the success they sought.

My efforts have been recognized by others. In the spring of 2016, I was recognized by the Solo and Small Firm Practice Division of the ABA with the "Solo and Small Firm Trainer Award" and in 2017 recognized by the State Bar of Michigan, Solo and Small Firm Section with the "Outstanding Achievement Award" for my efforts to help students and solo practitioners find success in practice.

Chapter 3

Why You Shouldn't Listen to Me

Which Path Is Right for You?

Believe nothing merely because you have been told it. Do not believe what your teacher tells you merely out of respect for the teacher. But whatsoever, after due examination and analysis, you find to be kind, conducive to the good, the benefit, the welfare of all beings—that doctrine believe and cling to, and take it as your guide.

Buddha

At the time of this writing, I have been publishing a blog for over eighteen months. If you follow it, I hope you have found it to be helpful. However, my ideas are my ideas, whereas you need to develop a practice that is well suited to your circumstances. That means that you will need to do all the work necessary for your success and create a practice that builds on your strengths and compensates for those aspects of your personality that are missing or weak. This will constantly challenge you and your ability to succeed in the business of law. There are many "coaches" out there who will offer to help you. But there are many who really don't know what they are talking about. Or they tell you, if you do this or that, you will be successful.

What follows is a quote from a blog called the Unwashed Advocate. In it, the author has a list intended to share ideas that the author feels someone in the practice of law needs to know. This list was first published after the author's first year of practice. Copied below is one of the elements of that list that I wish to share with you. His entire list is really good, too! But this bullet point explores the fact that no one, but you, can really determine the path you need to follow to be successful. It is also the reason I tell my students to go into the field and interview attorneys in their geographic area who are the same gender and the same ethnic background as themselves. I have them interview practicing lawyers with over ten years of experience and attorneys with less than three years of experience. You should also undertake this exercise to better understand the good, the bad, and the ugly of going solo before dipping your feet into those murky waters. The greater number of attorneys you interview, the better prepared you will be to handle the stress and realities of solo practice.

The author of the Unwashed Advocate says:

> *You're just as smart as self-titled gurus, business practice experts, SEO gurus, solo practice experts, and law office startup coaches, unless you hire them. I promise you, you are just as smart as any of these people. Like them, you can google business information and read about the ins and outs of starting your practice, building a business model, and attracting clients. The only way you are below them in expertise and intellect is if you hire them. Secondary note: if they have been licensed to practice law for less than 5 years, they have no business giving advice. They know precisely squat. Secondary secondary note: if they've never established their own long-term successful practice, they don't know anything more than you. Wake up. Spot these charlatans early and often.[1]*

Finding your own way is not an easy task and it takes work, but it is the only way to success. No one else can do this for you. It takes work. But, if you are willing to do the hard work, the payoff is great. The results will be worth the effort you put into it.

---

1. "The List," *Unwashed Advocate* (blog), November 7, 2011, https://unwashedadvocate.com/the-list.

Chapter 4

Your Chances of Going Solo Are Greater Than You Might Think

What they didn't tell you while you were in law school is that, eventually, there is a greater likelihood of you going solo, if not right out of law school, then into solo practice from a employment in the legal or government sector, than not.

If you are graduating from most law schools that are not classified as "top tier" law schools, or if you didn't graduate in the top 5 or 10 percent of your class, then you are more likely to end up in a small firm or solo setting after graduation than in a large firm practice setting. Why? Look at the demographics from an ABA compilation from 2015 concerning a survey of private practitioners. Since 1980, the number of solos as a percentage of the total appears to be relatively unchanged at 49 percent. But if you increase the number to attorneys in the 2–5 lawyer firm numbers, the percentage (small firm/solo) rises to 63. If you look at the other end of the spectrum, "101+ law firm lawyers" the numbers trend upward. What this means is that you are in the minority of practicing attorneys if you are in a large firm setting. Fewer seats at the top means statistically fewer chances of ending up in a large firm setting. This is particularly true if you are not one of the competitive graduates who are placed in the top 5 or 10 percent of their class. If you graduated in 2005, there was a 32 percent chance you would end up in a large firm setting (law firms with over eleven attorneys). Alternatively, there was almost a 63 percent chance you would not end up in a large firm and almost a 50 percent chance that you would end up in solo practice.[1]

---

1. http://www.americanbar.org/content/dam/aba/administrative/market_research/lawyer-demographics-tables-2015.authcheckdam.pdf.

Flip a coin and your odds are almost the same, solo versus not. So why take a chance of graduating without a backup plan that statistically is just as likely to occur as not? If you graduated in the bottom of your class, or if you didn't graduate from an elite law school, your chances of going solo are even greater. Keep in mind, I don't agree with employers who make their decisions primarily on law school attended or student rank. In fact, if you are unsuccessful finding employment in one of those "sweatshops," it may be the best thing that ever happens to you.

Or, consider a survey done by Robert Half Legal from May 19, 2016, which is a top placement firm for lawyers.

"Survey: Nearly One-Quarter of Lawyers Would Start Their Own Law Firm"

MENLO PARK, Calif., May 19, 2016 /PRNewswire/—Hanging out a shingle has become more attractive to lawyers, a new survey shows. Nearly one-quarter (23 percent) of lawyers interviewed by Robert Half Legal said they would establish a law firm if they had the necessary capital. These results represent an 18-point increase from a similar survey conducted in 2005, when just five percent of lawyers said they would open their own law office. Seventy-six percent of lawyers recently polled said they are not interested in starting a solo practice.

The survey was developed by Robert Half Legal, a legal staffing and consulting solutions firm specializing in lawyers, paralegals and other highly skilled legal professionals. It was conducted by an independent research firm and is based on 350 telephone interviews with lawyers in the United States and Canada: 175 of the respondents are employed at law firms with 20 or more employees and 175 are employed at companies with 1,000 or more employees.

Lawyers were asked, **"If you had the necessary capital, would you start your own law firm?"** Their responses:

	2016*	2005
Yes	23%	5%
No	76%	93%
Don't Know	2%	2%

*Total does not equal 100 percent due to rounding.

"Cloud computing platforms and mobile devices have made it easier to start an individual law practice with less capital investment—all you really need is a fully loaded laptop, a phone, an Internet connection and a workspace," said Charles Volkert, executive director of Robert Half Legal. "As the barriers to entry have been reduced, more people may be tempted to go into business for themselves, especially if they aren't feeling satisfied at their current company or law firm."

But Volkert cautioned, "Just because you can go solo doesn't mean you should. It takes an entrepreneurial mindset and a significant amount of time to develop a market presence and cultivate client relationships. It also means rolling up your sleeves to tackle administrative tasks, such as billing and calendaring, in addition to practicing law."[2]

---

2. "Survey: Nearly One-Quarter of Lawyers Would Start Their Own Law Firm," PRNewswire, May 19, 2016, http://www.prnewswire.com/news-releases/survey-nearly-one-quarter-of-lawyers-would-start-their-own-law-firm-300271562.html.

Chapter 5

The Dilemmas Law Students Face When Deciding to Practice Solo

The "Golden Handcuffs"

Many of those who work in law firms would prefer to be on their own. The lack of capital is one of the factors holding them back, but as the comments illustrate, you don't need a lot of capital to go out on your own. The real hold-up is the fact that most of those individuals getting a regular paycheck are dependent on that income to keep them solvent. Once you enter the world of corporate law firms, you soon find yourself assuming obligations; the mortgage, car payments, health insurance, and dependent family expenses. Go out on your own with those obligations tugging at your coattails, and you have very little choice.

Why the drastic change in attitude from 2005 to 2016 from lawyers working in large firms who wish they didn't? Could it be that associates are being asked to do more with less? Are the pressures even greater than in the past? Do the associates understand that with the technology available today that they can also be competitive with the large firms in many instances?

I recommend you "take the plunge" when you have fewer obligations and less to lose. That is, start out as a solo when you have greater flexibility. Don't wait until you are unable to break away.

So, it is almost as likely that you will end up going solo even if you don't start out that way based on surveys that show nearly half of all private practitioners are in solo practice. Many attorneys do not learn this lesson until it is too late. Many law students still have the vision of practicing in a large firm setting when they first go into practice. Most of them, in my opinion, are seeing the world through rose-colored glasses. If you are unsure of the outcome for yourself, then I invite you to follow along and engage in the program of self-exploration, which I detail in this book, while you are still in law school. In fact, even if you have no desire to go solo, and if you feel you are destined to end up in a large firm setting, I would still encourage you to create a business plan before you graduate as a backup plan for the possibility of solo practice. As you go through the process I outline in this book, I believe it will be transformational for you. And you may find that you change your mind as you go through that process. As my colleague, Professor Chris Trudeau once said to me, "Even in a large law firm you are a solo. If you can't operate independently and bring in business, you will not be retained."

But first you need to understand that finding a job with a large firm or even a medium-sized firm can be a difficult undertaking. Because of the competitive environment in law firm employment outcomes, if you didn't graduate in the top 5 percent of your class or from a top tier law school, you will find a great deal of prejudice against hiring you if you don't meet that criteria.

Why the Prejudice?

When hiring partners are faced with hiring decisions, they look for factors that predict success in practice. It is reasonable to assume that a student who does well academically has a gifted intellect. The hiring partners assume that he or she will grasp complex legal principles better than a student who struggled academically in law school. It would also be safe to assume that a gifted student would be a new associate whom the firm might convert from trainee (loss center) into a competent practitioner (profit center) more rapidly than someone who has not demonstrated intellectual prowess in the past. Even if that student had to work hard for the grades he or she got, all the better—as that demonstrates motivation and a work ethic that the firm can parlay into good revenue—as that new associate is probably going to be a workaholic, which translates into more billable hours. So GPA matters and your resume is used to *exclude* as many candidates as possible. This is so the hiring partner doesn't have to waste time meeting with numerous unqualified candidates. There is a simple mechanism used to disqualify you from the "interview this one" pile; it is called the disqualifying low GPA.

Elitism

Another method used to discriminate who is hired and who is not by the elite law firms is your school of origin. If you are not in the "first tier" classification of law schools according to U.S. News and World Report, then many firms will not bother to meet with you regardless of your academic standing. Welcome to the world of elitism. The reason for their prejudice is that they want to advertise to the world, a stable of attorneys with the right credentials when dealing with MBAs and others, themselves seeking the services of like-minded, status-sensitive lawyers. Again, I believe that you are really better off steering clear of organizations that place the weight of decision making on your GPA or school of origin as their primary consideration for new hires.

What you will find out soon after graduation is that GPA doesn't define you or your likely success in the practice of law. Many of my students in the clinic I supervise, who are not "academically gifted," perform just as well as students ranked well above them in their class. Work ethic and attention to detail, in my opinion, are much better predictors of success when evaluation factors predictive of success. If you go solo, you will find it to be extremely unlikely that your clients will ever ask you about your GPA or how well you performed on your law school exams. Why? Because, they know it doesn't matter. They will hire you based on your ability to instill confidence in them that you can do the job and your ability to connect with them to establish a bond and a relationship with them.

Historical Prejudice Institutionalized

Most classes are taught by professors whose academic credentials and own experiences were not established in solo or small firm settings. Many of them came right out of academia or worked as law clerks for appellate or supreme court justices and rarely had contact with clients in a solo or small firm setting. We tend to model that which we know best.

Most of your classes were taught using Socratic methods by exploring published cases from the appellate courts cleansed of the proceeding in the lower courts. So you only reviewed those cases that made it to the high court. Most of the practical implications of competing on a day-to-day basis for business by general practitioners was missing from your training during the first year of law school.

However, after completion of your required first-year classes, many of you took electives. Many of those classes were taught by adjuncts who came to class after a full day of practice in the trial courts or dealing with real client issues, which may or may not have resulted in litigation. It is likely that only then did you get to hear "war stories" about what it was like to practice law like most practitioners experience it. But most of those adjunct professors were not members of the curriculum committees of those law schools and didn't have much say in the evolution of the curriculum. So the full-time faculty, who were removed from the day-to-day operations of a struggling solo practitioner, failed to give those considerations much weight. Indeed, they failed to consider that most of the students that they were teaching would end up in practice settings that were foreign to their full-time professors. Thus, the emphasis on training students for the "real world" of practice remained virtually absent from the required course curriculum.

Economic Pressures and Competition for Law Firm Positions

Some of the preferential treatment of highly ranked law students, or high achievers, changed with the economic downturn in 2006 as many of the large firms were discharging long-term associates. That left new graduates (even those who did very well academically) with no alternative but to compete for the reduced number of job openings against seasoned and highly qualified attorneys who experienced a reduction in force (RIF), and were themselves in the hunt for the few employment opportunities.

Recent grads took to the Internet and expressed great dismay at having to seek employment when opportunities were few and far between. As a result, the number of recent graduates who previously would have found employment within a law firm found themselves going solo out of desperation and not by choice.

Law firms, in an attempt to reduce expenses and compete against a changing legal services delivery system, began to lose business to in-house counsel. Businesses wanted to control the cost of legal counsel, and the best way to do so was to hire their own attorneys.

This led to restructuring within the law firms and greater cost controls. This resulted in more calls for "practice ready" law students who could be turned around quickly from "loss centers" to "profit centers." As a result, more and more law schools who were trying to fill seats began to sing the praises of practice-ready graduates and offered more classes geared toward skills development. Many schools established "incubators" to give their grads a support system to help them transition into practice on their own.

Chapter 6

So What Are You Afraid of? Your Greatest Fear May Be Success

The way to develop self-confidence is to do the thing you fear and get a record of successful experiences behind you. Destiny is not a matter of chance, it is a matter of choice; it is not a thing to be waited for, it is a thing to be achieved.

William Jennings Bryant

I have heard, from someone who has experienced tremendous success in solo practice, that the greatest obstacle to your success or failure as an attorney in solo practice is your "fear of failure." Doing nothing guarantees failure. But I have also heard from another one of my former students, who has been very successful, that your greatest fear may be "your fear of success." What are you going to do if suddenly your door is crowded with clients seeking services that you have not done before? What if they ask questions about legal matters that you can't answer?

The solution, "I want to work for someone else to get experience before I go solo." I often hear this from my students. They say that fear of failure is not the issue, but that they need to learn how to practice law and if they work for someone else, they will get that training.

As another solo once told me, "Every day, I have a crisis of confidence." In other words, each day presents some new legal quandary that I have not dealt with before. It is true that by working for someone else you will gain experience. But you will also gain experience working for yourself. The difference is that you will gain experience working for someone else while you are being paid a fraction of what you can earn on your own doing the same work. Often your resources are going to be just as good, and many times better than if you are employed by someone else.

How Can I Say That?

The truth is that your experience working for someone else will be hard earned. It will not come easily when you are struggling to meet the minimum billable hours for your employer. Do you really think the partners in your office will be sitting by your side teaching you how to practice law step by step? When they are billing at $300 an hour and you are billing at $100 an hour, do you think they will be sitting by your side tutoring you? How much time do you think they will devote at the $100 rate which is what they will have to bill for your work product? It takes them away from doing their $300-an-hour work if they are tutoring you. They can't double bill. Plus, they are being held accountable for billable hours just like you. Where are they going to find the time to help you without sacrificing some of their time?

The new reality, even in the large and well-financed law firms, is that they are looking for "practice ready" lawyers to populate those firms. Sure, a few of the large firms will invest time and money in you—and they will invest time with some training. But are you graduating in the top of your class to land one of those jobs? If not, take a lesson from those who have been down a different road.

This is the new norm, first day for the new associate, after being escorted around the office to find the coffeemaker and restroom: "We have a hearing scheduled next week on a motion to dismiss. Here is the file, prepare a response." So you ask the paralegal for assistance and you are told by the paralegal, "Sorry, I am too busy, and I have minimum billable hours to produce, just like you. You went to law school and passed the Bar, figure it out." You ask for assistance from another junior associate. "Sorry, I have enough trouble meeting my required billable hours, and besides, I don't have any more experience than you. Go figure it out." (To herself, "Besides, I am competing against you, why should I help you?") So you do your best and present your work to your superior who proceeds to chew you out. He tells you that "We have deadlines to meet, get it done, and do it properly, do it over . . ." You soon find out that you will learn a great deal by osmosis and observing about the culture of the firm. But the substantive law, for the most part, will be gleaned from the practice manuals and research that you do on your own. And once you have a steady paycheck, you begin to acquire a car payment and a house payment, get married and become responsible for dependents who need medical insurance. Four years out when you have finally established yourself as a family law attorney with a good reputation and understanding of that area of practice, you are too far in debt to quit and go out on your own. So you look for someone on the outside to partner with you to help you restart and break free of the rat race so that you can have time with your family. Let's hope that your new partner will have the same work ethic as you and won't be on the golf course on Friday afternoon when you are completing a brief that is on deadline.

Here is another scenario that I want you to think about. Go solo right out of law school. Keep your overhead low and establish a business plan before you leave law school. I can help you do that in a way that will help you to succeed in the business end of this profession. You will also find out that there is help out there to get you acclimated to the practice principles and tools that you will need to be confident that your lack of experience will not hurt you. This book is a resource for materials, guidance, and information from some experts and lessons from those who failed so you know what not to do. It may surprise you, but in today's law firms, you must operate like a solo. If you can't work independently and develop business contacts, you will not be retained.

So if your feet will be held to that fire in a firm, why not fan a fire of your own? Go solo!

But I really believe that you don't fear failure—you fear success. As I heard Sarah Ostahowski (http://www.ski-law.com), a recent successful graduate, say, "Your real fear is what if you are successful and bring in a lot of clients—what do you do with all of them?" And she was right. Your real fear is success, not failure.

Chapter 7

Two Who Made the Plunge (Sarah/Alex)

I frequently have former students, who have gone solo, come to the law school to sit on a panel and invite students who are contemplating solo practice to come ask questions about how they did it. The panelists are instructed to do a short presentation about the good, the bad, and the ugly of going solo. In the past, I have used solos who have been in practice for some time. Then I started to rely on more recent grads to discuss the considerations of entering practice while servicing their student debt and entering the market at a time when the market is undergoing significant changes.

Those panels never fail to surprise the students in positive ways to help them gain confidence in going solo themselves. They also help the students to get a better sense of what they will encounter when they go into the field. Two former WMU Cooley students appeared together in the past, Sarah Osta-howski, PLC, http://www.ski-law.com/ of Shepherd, Michigan and Alex Benikov, http://www.benikovlaw.com/ of Phoenix, Arizona. I preserved an MP3 recording of their appearance. It lasted over two hours and I frequently give students who are considering solo practice access to that audio recording. Almost without exception, the feedback I get from the students who listen to it is that it is very revealing, surprising, informative, and encouraging. The presenters were out of law school about three years when they appeared on the panel. By that time, both of them had experienced significant success in practice. Of all the panelists I have sponsored, Sarah and Alex were two who, in my opinion, epitomized how students from diverse backgrounds can make it as solo practitioners.

Alex and Sarah come from different backgrounds. Alex, by his own admission, has the lowest LSAT score of anyone he has ever known. Alex graduated at the bottom of his class and he will proudly tell you about that. Sarah, by contrast, graduated near the top of her class and was a *Law Review* editor.

Thus, academically, the two of them are at opposite ends of the spectrum. Another obvious difference is that they are opposite genders. Alex established his practice in a large city, Phoenix, Arizona. Sarah chose to establish her practice in a rural village of only 2,000 residents in Shepherd, Michigan. Alex primarily practices criminal defense while Sarah specializes in estate planning. Finally, Sarah opened her practice the day after she was sworn in after passing the Bar. She left law school with a business plan she developed before graduating. Alex was unable to find employment as an attorney. He struggled working alternate employment and found a job ultimately at a bakery until he finally decided he had had enough. He decided to strike out on his own figuring he had little to lose and couldn't do much worse than unloading a bakery truck in ninety-degree heat under the Arizona sun.

They both graduated about the same time and both of them were finding excellent financial and professional success in their practices. Alex even had two books published within the first three years of his practice and was teaching law office management as an adjunct at one of the law schools in Arizona.

How did they do it? They both explained that they were willing to get up before their competition and work harder than anyone else. They both exuded the characteristics, which I call the Carnegie skills (discussed in more detail in Chapter 9). They had learned what it took to connect with their clients and others who had the ability to refer business to their practices. They limited the subject matter that they practiced and learned to reach out to other attorneys to find the resources that they would need. They were not afraid to break the mold and not do what other attorneys did; they created practices that addressed the needs of their potential clients and were consistent with their personal styles.

Sarah created a rural practice with a "homey" atmosphere and dressed in clothing that was consistent with a rural lifestyle. Alex sought criminal defense assignments and in the meantime, while he was waiting for assignments, he offered to appear on behalf of other attorneys at hearings when they were unable to attend. He made a point of telling other attorneys that he was available and sought that kind of work.

Both practices were very different and yet both were very successful. At the time Sarah appeared in her third year of practice she had two offices and four employees and was practically debt free.

Sarah and Alex demonstrated that there is no single formula for success. They both agreed that one of the biggest barriers to success was fear of failure. Sarah also spoke about the fear of success that many of you might have. What if you are wildly successful, what would you do if you had too much business? How would you handle it?

Without fail, those sessions with the students ran overtime and the questions just kept coming. And after those sessions, student comments and appreciation for the opportunity to learn from solo practitioners continued long after those meetings. On many occasions, I have brought attorneys to WMU Cooley to talk about their experiences establishing and growing their practices. The information they share is pure gold for the students who are in attendance. Everyone who participates as a presenter describes their experiences and tells the audience that it is hard work, but very worthwhile. They also explain that each of them have different approaches when finding success and that they all have different strengths and weaknesses that they need to overcome.

Chapter 8

Understanding Your Strengths and Weaknesses

First, be yourself.

OK, you can put away the suit.

Go to http://theissalawfirm.com/about-us/mark-issa/ and watch the videos posted there concerning the members of the Issa Law Firm. You will see the firm's attorneys profiled in ways that play to their natural strengths. Each profile highlights different aspects of each attorney's personality. These videos are exceptionally well done and will help those attorneys to appeal to many types of individuals.

The aspects of the individual personalities, although quite different from one another, are explored in ways that the viewer may be drawn to different attorneys based on the qualities that the potential client is seeking in their representation. These videos demonstrate how different personalities may appeal to different audiences. However, each will appeal to almost everyone because they are being true to themselves.

Think about your own characteristics. How do others perceive you? Are you a laid-back type of person? Are you driven? Do you obsess over detail? Are you a big picture person? Ask your friends and enemies how they view you and consider stepping into that role as you develop your marketing strategy. That is one approach.

Conversely, you may not want to project a certain persona as a strategy as you saw used in the Issa Law Firm video. Instead, you may wish to demonstrate skill and experience in specialized areas of the law or services designed to address the needs of a discrete audience. Your marketing may be targeted toward a particular ethnic population or the special needs of certain populations; for instance, the blind, military veterans, or parents with children who have special needs.

In my first meeting with students in my Estate Planning Clinic, they are instructed to be themselves and not to try to mold their behavior into a model that they perceived to be the template for a lawyer they observed on TV or in the movies. The key is to discover that your clients will accept you for who you are within limits. Of course, professional demeanor, a degree of humility, and empathy will always serve you well. All of our students are videotaped and we review those videos. The best interviews are the ones in which the student relaxes and tells the client that they are nervous and want to do a good job for the client. From the client's standpoint, they are meeting with someone who is highly educated and they are often intimidated. From the student's standpoint, they are nervous and afraid of making mistakes. Or, they fear that the client will discover that the student doesn't know everything.

To balance the equation, a simple exercise will allow you to get comfortable and let the client explore all of the concerns that they might have. Here is what you should do: LISTEN MORE AND TALK LITTLE. Simply ask the client to tell you about himself. And as he does, explore further with prompts such as "tell me more" or "really" or "that is interesting." By starting the interview using this technique, you can sit back and relax and let the client do what everyone likes to do—talk about himself.

As you listen to your client's story, try to find points of connection. For instance, if he says he is a Vietnam vet, as was your father, make it a point to disclose that. It will serve to change his perception of you a little bit. It is that perception that allows him to see that you are more connected than he realized before the conversation began. Keep listening. She has a dog, so do you. He is one of three children and the oldest, so are you. The more you explore, the greater the likelihood that you will perceive one another very differently than when the conversation began. And the best part is that you got to sit back and let them do the talking. By the time they have finished, you can now relax and be yourself. They no longer see you as someone on a pedestal. They will be more inclined to reveal more detail than before the conversation as they see you as more alike than dissimilar. You have now established a PERSONAL RELATIONSHIP.

That relationship and bonding is essential if you want return business and referrals from that client. What many attorneys fail to understand is that your current client base has the best potential to increase your business of any other efforts that you might engage in to market your firm. There is nothing stronger than a personal referral to convince someone that you are well qualified and worth your fee.

This process requires you to put yourself in the background and to make the client the center of attention. Once you have established connections, it is much easier for you to be yourself and for the client to accept you for who you are. Don't try to act like a lawyer. If you do, you are more likely to end up struggling to make ends meet. Most important, be true to yourself, be sincerely interested in your client's story, and return their phone calls. I believe you will be successful no matter what area of law you choose to practice and your business will grow and your client will learn to love you for who you are.

Chapter 9

What Really Matters: The Six Characteristics of Successful Solos

Perseverance alone does not assure success. No amount of stalking will lead to game in a field that has none.

I Ching

Practice doesn't make perfect! Every book that has been written, every lesson taught has the potential to help you improve the bottom line and your ability to succeed in practice. But, and here is the catch, you can't teach talent!

True Story

I watched with amazement, a program that featured a twelve-year-old playing the piano. Not only did this youngster play complex compositions on the piano, but he improvised and took many of those compositions to a higher level to the total shock and awe of all.

We sometimes see genius that seems to come from nowhere. That child was given a keyboard at age four, and he immediately started playing as if he were the reincarnation of a former musician. He had the gift! I have been trying to teach myself keyboard and guitar to keep my brain active in an effort to be sharp mentally as I age. I have attempted to master some of the technical skills to replicate the work of others. I enjoy the process. But I cannot break away from the technical strictures that I impose on myself to develop the skills necessary to replicate what I have heard others perform perfectly with seeming abandon.

Some of my students go solo and have done exceeding well. Others have not. Many are struggling but keep getting better as they learn from their successes and failures. Yet some are wildly successful. The materials I provide are the same. The coaching is pretty much the same. The tools that I provide are the same. Yet some outperform others by a wide margin. Why?

Talent cannot be taught. Skills can be developed and techniques taught, but talent—that is another matter. Some of my students appear to have been born with the "Carnegie" skills as I like to call them. That is, they interact with everyone in a manner that just draws those individuals to them. They are like "human magnets." I have a colleague like that. His office is always busy with students, professors, even maintenance personnel stopping in just to say "hello." People like him. My door, by contrast, has hinges that are not well worn. He has the Carnegie skills. Everybody feels like he is a great friend because he emanates warmth and empathy. It isn't artificial. It is just the way he is. He was born with it.

There are several characteristics that I can point to that thematically seem to appear in those individuals who have successful businesses. They really cannot be taught. They must be cultivated or augmented in some manner by those who don't have those natural talents.
What are they?

- Interpersonal skills
- Imagination and creativity
- Natural enthusiasm
- Work ethic
- Ability to organize to get things done
- Fearlessness

You can get by if one or more of these natural talents are missing from your personal inventory. However, if all or most of them are missing from your personality, you may be better served by finding employment with another. Some of my students come to that conclusion after interviewing multiple solo practitioners. You may associate with another attorney who is a "task master" to substitute for work ethic. You may seek the assistance of others to help you come up with ideas to market yourself or promote your business to help you with creativity. You may use various tools available to help you become better organized. But if you are deficient in all of these areas, you may want to look for a job where the business of that organization is not dependent on you for its existence.

Few of my students possess all of these characteristics. And, even if they possess all of them, some are stronger than others. But the ones who do possess all of them, to some degree, really do not need my assistance. But they still seek my guidance to enhance their natural talents. I get it, so do they. Do you? Consider, with some rigor, whether you are really cut out to go into business for yourself. If not, "Plan B" may be in order.

The Six Characteristics of Successful Solos

I will be discussing each characteristic in detail below, and how you might deal with deficiencies in any of these areas. Even though these characteristics might not come naturally, they can be enhanced or compensated to some extent. Do an honest self-assessment and determine whether, after reviewing each of these essential characteristics, you have it in you to go into business for yourself.

1. Fearlessness

You'll always miss 100% of the shots you don't take.

Wayne Gretzky

If you find that you are like most people and don't possess all of the six qualities, can you adapt and compensate to overcome your shortcomings?

Fear is natural. We all look for predictability and prefer to maintain the status quo. Fear can be very beneficial, or paralyzing, depending on how you deal with your fear. All business is about risk. The following quote from the *Harvard Business Review* helps put into perspective the difference between risk-averse behavior that is advantageous versus that kind of behavior that is short-sighted and destructive.

> When Tony Hayward became CEO of BP, in 2007, he vowed to make safety his top priority. Among the new rules he instituted were the requirements that all employees use lids on coffee cups while walking and refrain from texting while driving. Three years later, on Hayward's watch, the Deepwater Horizon oil rig exploded in the Gulf of Mexico, causing one of the worst man-made disasters in history. A U.S. investigation commission attributed the disaster to management failures that crippled "the ability of individuals involved to identify the risks they faced and to properly evaluate,

communicate, and address them." Hayward's story reflects a common problem. Despite all the rhetoric and money invested in it, risk management is too often treated as a compliance issue that can be solved by drawing up lots of rules and making sure that all employees follow them. Many such rules, of course, are sensible and do reduce some risks that could severely damage a company. But rules-based risk management will not diminish either the likelihood or the impact of a disaster such as Deepwater Horizon, just as it did not prevent the failure of many financial institutions during the 2007–2008 credit crisis.[1]

These are the kind of organizational risk adverse protocols that can lead to unintended consequences. In the same way, many of the students and practitioners I see engage in a strategy as perverse as that which led to the BP catastrophe.

Instead of the lids on coffee cups, many new graduates seek cover under the letterhead of an experienced attorney to "learn the ropes" before going out on their own. They feel they will find out how to practice law under another attorney's shadow. Indeed, they find a path. But it is often not the one intended. Instead, they end up "shoehorning" themselves into the pattern and style of practice dictated by their superior. They are told to take charge of a family law file and complete the work in that case. If the new graduate's passion is really estate planning, it is, more likely than not, that they will be told to work on some other area of law. So they submit and complete those matters as assigned. They do it in lockstep with the senior attorney's orders. If the senior attorney is aggressive, they will be expected to be aggressive and assume the mantle of persona that that attorney projects. Soon they find that they are attempting to be a "mini-he" or "mini-she" and lose all perspective of who they want to be or how they would like to practice law.

The fear of going it alone has trapped you into believing that the only way to practice is the way you were taught. If you rebel and decide that you no longer want to take orders from someone else, and go out on your own, you have spent valuable time waiting to reset your clock and start all over again. We often see this with large firm associates leaving after a couple of years after being burned out.

Where is the greatest risk? Putting yourself out there and doing your very best. Seek the advice of other experienced practitioners. If you work through

---

1. Robert S. Kaplan and Anette Mikes, "Managing Risks: A New Framework," *Harvard Business Review*, June 2012, https://hbr.org/2012/06/managing-risks-a-new-framework.

each case, learning as you go, you will find your way. Malpractice insurance is cheap when you first start out. And it is essential to give you greater confidence. It allows you to have someone "watching your back." There is no lack of resources available for you to gain experience. You will often find that other solo practitioners will be more generous with their time than attorneys employed in large firms. The solo's time is his or her own. Solos will empathize with you. The good ones will not see you as competition. The bad ones, who won't give you the time of day, are not worth learning from anyway.

Working for someone else also leads to financial dependency. Suppose you find yourself in a firm where you are treated with respect? Even in a firm that gives you some choice about what kind of law you can practice and a firm that provides a generous and predictable income, it can become the "golden handcuffs." What if soon after starting work in that firm, you purchase a house? And you buy a car, then you get married. You have children. Your financial obligations mitigate against departure. Because you cannot survive without that regular income. So you stick it out. Even though you might wish you could leave, you can't.

During the financial collapse of 2005, many attorneys found themselves with few options after being discharged. There is no such thing as job security. The only employer you can really count on is YOU!

However, your fears are real. How do you deal with them? As a recent graduate, consider what you have to risk. My former private investigator, Vic Hedges, used to say, "you can't fall off the floor." He said this when we took cases to trial when the prosecutor wasn't willing to consider a reasonable deal for our clients. The same is true for many of you who are recent grads. What do you have to lose? If you have student debt, the lender can defer those loans (at a cost), but they can be deferred. Your greatest risk is inactivity and failing to take action. If you cannot handle that fear, and you will freeze, then maybe finding employment with someone else makes sense. But, time after time, I have had former graduates tell me that they were glad they took the risk of going it alone. It paid dividends in terms of control over their lives. It paid dividends financially over time. And most of them tell me that they are much better off financially than they would have been working for someone else after a few years of practice.

The best way to conquer your fear is to visit other solo practitioners in your area and find out how they did it. Ask them about the good, the bad, and the ugly of going solo. Establish a business plan based upon the demographics and demand for quality services that others are not providing.

Establish relationships with good practitioners to mentor you as you develop your practice. Do the things you are passionate about. Get up before everyone else and work long into the night investing your energy to build the best practice possible and YOU WILL SUCCEED. Conquer your fears and move forward.

2. Imagination and Creativity

Fantasy, abandoned by reason, produces impossible monsters, united with it, she is the mother of the arts and the origin of marvels.

Francisco de Goya

By the time you graduate from law school, most of the imagination and creativity has been drummed out of you. Why? Because the principle purpose of law school is to train you to "think like a lawyer"!

What does that mean? It means that you put the imagination and creative skills aside. Skills that you have exercised all of your life have no place in doctrinal law. We are looking for an application of the rules to the fact pattern presented without all the fluff. "Just the facts, ma'am, just the facts!," as Sergeant Joe Friday on Dragnet was often heard to say. That is what we were taught. No more creativity. The rules are the rules. The logic is clear and the reasoned opinions need not be cluttered up with your imaginings.

There were timed exams with strict rules to be applied almost scientifically. Yes you could end up reasoning different results or outcomes, but if you went off on a tangent inventing new concepts based on changes in the law, you got an "F." So, enough of that free thinking; you need to think like a lawyer. And so it goes. Three years of having that drummed into your head and you soon forget what it is like to dream or conjure up creative ways to find recourse for your client.

How do you break free from the strictures and paradigms learned? Well, it isn't easy and not everyone can be cured. Go amongst your brother lawyers and see how they are doing it—then do it differently! Don't do what other lawyers do or you will be doomed to follow in their path of mediocrity. Of course, there are exceptions. For every lawyer who has a fixed practice, using standard techniques for marketing and management, you will find the few who have found a different path and also met with success. Find them and use them to get excited about the opportunities available for you as well if you will just look around.

Often nonlawyers can be a great source of ideas as can the Internet. Here are a few ideas on how you might stimulate your own creativity.

- Go to the Internet and search terms related to the topic you are considering. "Marketing," client management, accounting for lawyers, latest trends, discussion groups, and so forth.
- Go for a run or other exercise without the headset and wear earplugs. As you exercise, often you will have ideas that can be transcribed to your phone with a recorder application on your smartphone.
- Take a drive, a long drive, and keep your recorder handy to record your ideas.
- Attend marketing and business development seminars or the local Chamber of Commerce meetings. Tell them what you are attempting to accomplish and ask for ideas on how you might solve your problems.
- Pet your dog with a notepad handy. Often some of the best ideas come when we are attentive to others and disassociated from the demands placed upon us.
- Engage in a hobby that you enjoy. I like to work with stained glass and often during the process of mechanically fitting pieces together, I have to release myself from the mental gymnastics required to resolve legal issues. My hobby requires concentration, but of a different kind and requires a different part of the brain to function successfully. It is often during those times that some of my best ideas come to me.
- Read. Find materials that are on the Internet or books that you wanted to read but never had the time. Don't weigh yourself down reading every word. Read in "express mode." By that, I mean read the first sentence of every paragraph. Often it will convey the author's intent sufficiently that you get the idea and move through the book more rapidly. Of course, read every word that I write in this book! (just kidding) You can cover more territory that way. Finally, read the summary at the end of the book. Read the great idea books. Go to the local bookstore and pick through the self-help books. Use the express reading process described above, get a cup of coffee and keep your recorder app active as you do to record the ideas you get from your readings.
- One great idea borrowed from the website MaRS is about "keeping a "pain point" journal.

"Successful companies all have one thing in common: they solve a problem. Companies like Google, Netflix, and Uber solved specific pain points in their marketplace and went on to achieve great things. I wish I could find information on a specific topic from various sources quickly. I wish I could rent movies and television shows directly from my television at a low cost. I wish there was a cheaper way to get a ride. Ask yourself: What bugs me? Keep a journal where you write down your everyday frustrations. Review the journal regularly and run it by others to see if it's a pain point for them. What product or service could you create that would solve that problem?"[2]

As you review your own legal services, what are the pain points for your clients or clients of other law firms?

- Conduct surveys of your clients or others in your industry to ask them for ideas to provide better services at a lower cost point.
- Go to https://www.cleverism.com/18-best-idea-generation-techniques to learn eighteen killer idea-generation techniques, including SCAMPER:

    SCAMPER is an idea-generation technique that utilizes action verbs as stimuli. It is a well-known kind of checklist developed by Bob Eberie that assists the person in coming up with ideas either for modifications that can be made on an existing product or for making a new product. SCAMPER is an acronym with each letter standing for an action verb which in turn stands for a prompt for creative ideas.
    S—Substitute
    C—Combine
    A—Adapt
    M—Modify
    P—Put to another use
    E—Eliminate
    R—Reverse (for instance, use this to reverse the result you seek for ideas—what would I have to do to have no clients?)[3]

Try some of these techniques and see if they help to get the creative juices flowing again. It can be hard at times to invest your energy into this type of planning. But, it can provide significant opportunities for growth and

---

2. Jelena Djurkic, "7 Ways to Generate Business Ideas This Year," *MaRS* (blog), December 16, 2014, https://www.marsdd.com/news-and-insights/seven-ways-to-generate-business-ideas.
3. "18 Best Idea Generation Techniques," *Cleverism* (blog), May 14, 2015, https://www.cleverism.com/18-best-idea-generation-techniques.

profitability. Let me share just two ideas that my students have come up with or discovered when visiting other solo practitioners. In addition to specializing in estate planning for pets as mentioned in a later section of this book, you might consider what one student proposed. She considered becoming a "full-timer" and doing estate planning for other full-timers.

A full-timer is an individual who lives full-time in an RV rather than a fixed location. There are many retirees who fill that bill and travel with the seasons. She proposed setting up an office in her RV, which doubled as her home. A side benefit was that significant portions of her home/office would be tax-deductible. She would take the Bar in a northern and also in a southern state. In the summer months, she would stay in the north and rent a spot where others recreate and offer her services to those individuals. She would gear her estate planning practice to the needs of individuals who had no fixed address and did everything on the Internet. She would do home visits for home-bound seniors and in the winter, she would go south doing the same type of work assisting many of the same clients as they translocated. With the Internet, you can practice from anywhere. Try to do that in a large firm setting!

Another clever use of the Internet was a fairly new attorney who practiced immigration law. She was unfamiliar with immigration law, but she linked up with a paralegal who was bilingual. The paralegal had over twenty years' experience in immigration law. Immigration law is often helping people fill out forms properly. So, much of her practice centered on services that were "unbundled"; that is, they were broken down into components that the client could select as needed. Many of the processes were simplified, yet required assistance, especially for those for whom English was a second language. The paralegal could interpret. The paralegal trained the new attorney and soon the attorney found that she could Skype clients wherever they were located. That meant she would Skype clients who were out of state since immigration law is Federal. Once a member of the Federal Bar, she could advise clients in virtually any state. Although the cost per transaction was less than full service, the attorney could meet the needs of numerous clients and with volume, she found that she was very busy and profitable.

If you go to www.ShopABA.org, you will find a series of books available on many topics. The list includes

The Little Book of Golf Law, Second Edition
The Little Book of Elvis Law
The Little Book of Skiing Law

The Little Book of Fitness Law
The Little Book of Horse Racing Law
The Little Book of Holiday Law
The Little Red Book of Wine Law
The Little Book of Coffee Law
The Little Book of Hunting and Fishing Law
The Little Book of Cowboy Law
The Little Book of Movie Law
The Little Book of Foodie Law
The Little Book of Music Law
The Little Book of Fashion Law
The Little Book of Boating Law
The Little Book of Space Law
The Little Book of BBQ Law
The Little Book of Basketball Law
The Little White Book of Baseball Law

As you look at the topics, it should be apparent to you that there are many ways that one can be creative in the practice of law. Many of these are written more for entertainment than as instructional manuals on how to establish a practice in BBQ law, for instance. However, as you review this list, keep in mind that your imagination and creativity are the only limitation to the object of your practice.

Consider tailoring your practice to a specific population with unique demands. Where do those people congregate, what do they read, with whom do they associate? As you consider those factors, keep in mind that the more you narrow your field of practice, the more you will find it possible to gain expertise in that area of law. As you do, you will be in a better position to charge fees commensurate with your knowledge. As I discuss in subsequent chapters, finding a niche—which requires imagination and creativity—can foster much greater efficiency in practice and ultimately greater profitability.

Even if you are not currently the most creative thinker who you know, you can enhance your skills by practicing some of the techniques listed above. You can also augment your skills with the assistance of others who have the "creative gene." This is one quality that requires cultivation and constant attention. But, if you do it and do it well, you will find you practice your passion and "work" as we know it will become something that other people do. Not you!

3. Work Ethic

In reading the lives of great men, I found that the first victory they won was over themselves . . . self-discipline with all of them came first.

Harry S. Truman

This is the hard one. As I have blogged in the past, many of our children are "victims of our success." That is not a term I created, but it certainly paints the picture that we all see all too often.

Nothing in the world can take the place of persistence. Talent will not, nothing is more common than unsuccessful men with talent. Genius will not; unrewarded genius is almost a proverb. Education will not; the world is full of educated derelicts. Persistence and determination are omnipotent.

Calvin Coolidge

My children were raised on a farm and had regular chores. They were responsible for the livestock to make sure that they were fed and watered properly. They cleaned stalls and helped collect eggs and helped during the birthing process. They were expected to work and engage in some sort of productive enterprise. So too, when I was a child, as one of twelve children, I was expected to be engaged in some sort of meaningful enterprise from the age of ten. From a paper route to a job as a caddy on a golf course and ultimately to work in a grocery store, I have worked some sort of job for my entire life.

Recently I watched a five-year-old being served special meals that were different from the adults because she "won't eat what we eat." I know of adolescents who demand that they be able to participate in soccer, football, basketball, hockey on travel teams that cause the parents great difficulty and expense. They have expensive equipment that costs more than many of the household appliances. And the parents of these children transport them day and night all year round to those events. Not once would they think of those children finding a job to offset some of those expenses. The children dominate their parent's lives. There is nothing wrong with being a dedicated parent. However, it is one thing to be doing this as the parent in control. It is altogether different to be doing this because the child is in control and directs the activities of the parent. The attitude and expectations of some of the students who I see do not align with my expectations or experiences growing up. We had to have jobs like paper routes, in grocery stores, or other summer jobs. Not any more. . . .

So now, as educators, we see those children graduate into the upper echelons of scholarly matriculation. As we do, it is apparent to us that the new generations—"Xers," "millennials," and "Zers"—do not have the work ethic that was more apparent in my generation (see below):[4]

Generation Name	Births Start	Births End	Youngest Age Today*	Oldest Age Today*
The Lost Generation - The Generation of 1914	1890	1915	102	127
The Interbellum Generation	1901	1913	104	116
The Greatest Generation	1910	1924	93	107
The Silent Generation	1925	1945	72	92
Baby Boomer Generation	1946	1964	53	71
Generation X (Baby Bust)	1965	1979	38	52
Generation Y - The Millennial - Gen Next	1980	1995	22	37
Generation Z	1996	2010	7	21
Gen Alpha	2011	2025	1	6

What happened? In some sense, I have heard it said, that "our children are victims of our success."

Children of my generation (boomers) raised our children differently. But we always wanted our children to do better than ourselves. Many of the parents of millennials seem to have forgotten what they went through. Seeking greater opportunities for their children, we seem to have forgotten why the "greatest generation" was great. It wasn't because they were coddled. It wasn't because they were raised to believe they should all be selected in every game and win a trophy for just being there. No, it was because many of them grew up under stress and they learned to deal with it. It was the norm. Today, our children rarely know what stress really is. There is an exception to this rule, however. And, I predict that if you are the exception, you will be exceptional.

---

4. http://www.careerplanner.com/Career-Articles/Generations.cfm.

The exceptions are those children growing up in poverty, or under stress with a drug addicted parent, living in foster homes, or being abused. Although, that may cause even greater problems. The truth is that some stress, some resourcefulness on the part of an adolescent in attempting to compensate, is not necessarily all bad. I am not suggesting that this is a good thing, but sometimes these children are actually better equipped to handle stress later in life than those children raised in perfect conditions. The child who was always picked for a team and always won a trophy for just being there will eventually grow up. When that child is confronted with stress, real stress, for the first time, he or she will fall apart. It is endemic in education now. It will get worse as those who were not stressed in their youth continue to matriculate through graduation and find themselves in the business world. No one will offer to fix them a "special meal" because they can't play by the rules of the rest of the world. Each of our children is special and will not be affected by the demands of society. He or she will prevail and go to the best schools with full scholarships and be the leader in their field. My child will be the CEO and everyone will play according to my child's rules.

The world is full of willing people; some willing to work, the rest willing to let them.

Robert Frost

I can teach skills, but I can't teach talent. Work ethic cannot be taught. It must come from within. When someone is subjected to stress throughout their lives or has been held to high standards of production, I might expect an outcome to match their conditioning. I have often seen this in first generation immigrant children. Parents come to the United States and establish businesses. Their children work in the business and those children do not want to work for someone else. They want to be their own boss and run their own business. It has been all they have experienced in life so far. Why should it be different?

Of all the other characteristics that I will be discussing, this is the most difficult. Most, if not all of the other characteristics of success can be compensated for in their absence. But not work ethic. Either you have it or you don't. One way to guarantee drive and motivation is if the subject matter you practice is your PASSION. If not, it will be a struggle. My advice on this one is to check yourself. If you are not willing to get up before everyone else and work later than your competition—find another line of work or work for someone else. But don't expect to succeed in your own solo practice.

4. Ability to Get Things Done

The person who makes a success of living is the one who sees his goal steadily and aims for it unswervingly.

Cecil B. DeMille

This is a critical attribute for those I see who find success in solo practice. You can have all the other characteristics and muddle through, but if you are not organized and capable of getting things done, you are destined to find yourself in a world of hurt. Time management is further addressed in Chapter 10.

I find the great thing in this world is not so much where we stand, as in what direction we are moving—we must sail sometimes with the wind and sometimes against it—but we must sail, and not drift, nor lie at anchor.

Oliver Wendell Holmes, Jr.

Of all the characteristics that I see in successful solos, this one is the one that is most easily taught, but once learned it must become habitual. That is, it must be designed so that one cannot miss the objective of all our planning. The objectives are the goals that we have made for ourselves. You must have a plan and not simply "drift nor lie at anchor." The problem with many students who I encounter is that they have never had to have a plan—unless they come from the world of business. And few of them have really set goals for themselves.

The first class I conduct with all my students includes a lesson on time management. You will never accomplish your goals unless you set them in the first instance. And you will never reach those goals without a plan and a method of executing on that plan.

For as long as I can remember, when I am in a meeting where the participants know me well, and resource information is sought—inevitably, they point to me and ask me to provide it. This is because I have an information management system that they know they can rely on for the answers. This started when I was still in sales and traveling over 100,000 miles a year over six states with responsibility for numerous dealers all over those states. I started using the Franklin Covey® time management system. Before computers, I used its paper calendar and task list system which was contained in a leather binder with compartments for my checkbook, stamps, and other important documents. Using that system, first, I set long-term and short-term goals. From there I learned several techniques to ensure that I didn't miss appointments or tasks that were assigned by others or self-delegated.

When I teach time management, I utilize concepts I learned under the Franklin Covey system. First, get a system. It can be paper based, electronic, or a combination of the two. Most important, get a system that you will use. I currently use my smartphone. Two important components of any system are a calendar and a task list.

Second, carry it with you always. The purpose for having it with you always is to take note of tasks AS THEY ARE ASSIGNED. Do not rely on your memory to record information later. As I say, write it down so you can FORGET ABOUT IT. You cannot possibly retain every single detail of every task when you practice law. There are too many cases with too many separate tasks associated with each one that are easily forgotten. Take the stress out of your memory and make a note of each task as it arises. Once it has been recorded you need to follow the next rule, and that is your "tickler."

Third, every day, at a time convenient for you, set aside twenty to thirty minutes and plan your day ahead. Turn off the phone, close the door, and DO NOT CHECK YOUR EMAILS. Look at the tasks you wrote down the day before and address them in order of importance. Use the "Eisenhower" planning technique. Rarely are important things urgent and rarely are the urgent things the most important. If an item is urgent and will be missed if the deadline is not met, place it high on the list of priorities. Use three categories: *critical*—must complete today, *important*—try to complete if at all possible today, and finally *as time allows*—for those tasks that need attention but are not time sensitive. After you have triaged those tasks, subgroup them and prioritize those subgroups. Finally, after establishing those three categories, review them for urgency and importance and reorder as necessary.

Many times during the day you may be interrupted to undertake a task that someone else feels is urgent. If it isn't important, don't be distracted from your scheduled tasks; stay on point. If you train others to respect your time, you will find that they will be less inclined to interrupt you. "I'm sorry, but I am scheduled to do _____ this hour. I will take note of your concern and get to it when I can schedule it into my calendar." This will have the effect of putting people off initially, but will pay dividends later when they find that you complete their task with greater efficiency than they anticipated. They will only respect your time if you do as well.

Also, a task might be so large that it defies completion in a day or even more. For the larger tasks, I recommend breaking them into twenty- to thirty-minute components. Pace yourself and spread them out over days, weeks, or even months with a target date for completion of the entire project. That way you will be making steady progress and meet your deadline.

Fourth, get one and only one system. The minute you try to keep two calendars or different task lists, or Post-it® Notes to track your tasks, you lose your ability to track events or tasks with complete confidence and will not be able to rely upon the system you have created.

Finally, use it for a minimum of eight weeks. Studies have shown that after doing something consistently for eight weeks, it will become a habit.

Use this system and I believe you will find life goes much smoother for you and you will reach your daily, weekly, monthly, annual, and long-term goals with greater efficiency. Finally, you will be able to sleep at night without the worry associated with thoughts that you might be forgetting something. Create a system, use the system, and if you do, you can "Forget About It" because it has all been captured and dealt with.

So, for the characteristic we see in others who have the "Ability to Get Things Done," you now know the secret to your own success. Implement it today and start on the path to reach your goals, whatever they are.

5. Natural Enthusiasm

Dance as if no one's watching, sing as if no one's listening, and live everyday as if it were your last.

Irish Proverb

This is another of those characteristics that is not easily taught, if at all. We all know people who constantly see the world as a "cup half full" and those who see it as a "cup half empty." What is the difference and why is it that some people are far more optimistic about life than others?

I do know this: without some enthusiasm for what you are doing, you will be destined to despair and make those close to you wish that they had greater distance from you. One remedy for lack of enthusiasm is to find something you are passionate about and make that your practice area. I referenced above the "Little Book Series" from the ABA as one way for you to explore your own potential and creativity by designing your practice to coincide with your personal interests.

What are your hobbies? What causes do you really believe in? What makes you angry where you see injustice? What population do you feel is neglected or disenfranchised? Where can you make a difference in the world with your knowledge of the law? Look around you and often you will find a cause or interest that ignites your instincts and excites you because of the possibilities.

Later in this book, I describe a friend of mine, Julie Ferstman, who had horses before she attended law school. While in law school, Julie decided to try and connect her interest in horses to her legal career. She began to look for anything related to horses in the Michigan statutes and case law. Soon she offered to write a monthly column for *Saddleup Magazine*, which is a periodical distributed to horse owners and others in Michigan and the surrounding states. Julie consistently wrote a column in that magazine about anything to do with horses and the law. What liability does one have for those who ride horses on their property? Who is liable when transporting horses? What considerations does one need to address when leasing a horse? She wrote on these topics and many more. As she did, she began to get referrals and requests for representation for horse-related matters. Before long, she was known as the "Equine Law Specialist." The last time we spoke, I believe about 60 percent of her practice was devoted to Equine Law. She is also a frequent speaker throughout the United States concerning Equine Law. She is also the recent past president of the State Bar of Michigan. She started as a solo practitioner with an interest and parlayed it into her practice specialty.

Think in your own life what might be an interest that you might convert into your practice area. If you find the key to that interest and leverage your personal knowledge and insight into a specialized practice area, I believe you will be naturally enthusiastic about what you do. I have been fortunate to have a job where I teach in a clinical program designed to help students learn how to effectively communicate with clients and gain experience providing legal advice even before they graduate and pass the Bar.

6. Interpersonal Skills (Carnegie Skills)

One reason why birds and horses are not unhappy is because they are not trying to impress other birds and horses.

Dale Carnegie

How do you feel when going to a gathering with people you have never met before? Are you uncomfortable? Do you retreat to a corner somewhere avoiding contact at all costs with the larger group? Well, you might be surprised to find that you are not afflicted with personal insecurities that are different from everyone else. In fact, most people do not like crowds and are not the life of the party wherever they go.

The interpersonal skills I feel are important are not the social skills that find you entertaining everyone you are with, with your humor, wit, and brilliant ideas. When I say interpersonal skills, I mean the ability to connect with clients in a way that comes naturally. Dale Carnegie wrote, *How to Win Friends and Influence People*, first published in 1936 and has sold over 10 million copies. In it, he provides tips on how to interact with others in a way that you focus on them in the course of your engagement. Really, that is the essence of the book. It is also the basis of establishing long-term and sustainable relationships with your clients.

I have heard of the "25/75 rule" when communicating with clients. What it means is that you should be talking no more than 25 percent of the time and the client should be talking 75 percent of the time when you meet them.

The interpersonal skills I see are the abilities to connect with clients, other legal professionals, and the public at large when engaging them. You know the people who possess those qualities. They are the individuals who make you feel at ease whenever you are around them. They are never trying to "one up" everyone else and allow others to dominate the conversation. Everyone feels they are one of that person's best friends. When you have problems, you can go to them and discuss those problems without being made to feel that your problems will be telegraphed to everyone you know.

Carnegie described principles in his book on how to persuade others to your way of thinking by listening to others with sincere interest and without criticizing or challenging their viewpoint. The methods he describes are viewed by critics as being outdated and too simplistic. One of the fundamental precepts of the book involves seeing things from the perspective of others and not from your viewpoint. This is one of the critical lessons of the book and a theme that runs through it. It is also one of the critical lessons that every lawyer needs to learn and implement when dealing with her clients.

One of the early lessons I try to teach my students is how to allow the client the freedom to speak freely about the reasons he is seeking your services. Open-ended questions need to be employed to allow the client to take the interview sequence where he feels he needs to take it. I tell my students to be curious and look for openings to ask the client to explore, in more detail, the facts that they wish to reveal and to allow the client to tell her story without interruption. The added advantage of allowing the client to tell that story is to allow you to make connections with the client. Rarely will their story fail to describe details from the client's background that parallel some aspect of your own life. His father retired from the Air Force, you were an officer in the Air Force. Connections like that will make you more "like" your client than before your conversation began. The more you are perceived as similar to one another, the greater chance you will be able to connect and establish a relationship with that client as opposed to a one-off service arrangement. Having good interpersonal skills is critical to establishing long-term client relationships and building a following. Very often, excellent interpersonal skills will outweigh your technical skills in the eyes of the client and be the difference between a growing, thriving practice and one that stagnates.

Chapter 10

Time Management

I can give you guidance and provide a systematic approach so that you can set the stage for your success later. What I cannot do is move you forward to execute on that plan. No amount of wishing or thinking alone will get it done. You can let the work control you, or you can control the work; it is up to you. This may be the most critical component of the plan that determines your success or failure. Take heed and listen up—or you will be destined to fail. Read on.

In the previous chapter, I outlined the six characteristics that I often see in successful solos. One of those characteristics was the ability to get things done. In that section, I outlined a process that I return to below as it is important that you do this or you are destined to mediocrity in the practice of law at best and doomed to malpractice at worst.

Also, in the last chapter, you were directed to go to court to find out what lawyers do so that you can better define the areas of practice that you might be interested in pursuing. I also encouraged you to expand your "universe" of contacts to seek out those who have the capacity to influence others to consider you as having expertise in areas of the law that others have not even considered. In Chapter 9, I also referenced attorneys who were prepared and organized and those who were not. The difference between the two is proper management of time and resources verses putting fires out as they arise.

How many of you read the first and second chapters, but have not taken active steps to follow through with my suggestions? If you are like most people, you read the material and thought, "that is a good idea, I will do that later."

I just met with a student who was having problems completing his work on time. As a result, he was facing academic disciplinary procedures. To forestall further problems, when we met, I assisted him in developing a method to plan ahead by setting goals, by documenting tasks as they arose, prioritizing those tasks, and ensuring follow-through to complete those tasks. We discussed using triggers to prompt him consistently and progressively until he completed his tasks. We refer to those as "ticklers." Before he left, he thanked me. This was the first time anyone had discussed and outlined a process that he could use.

I frequently see two types of problems when individuals fail to keep appointments or get their work done on time. The first is the failure to document or keep track of assignments. The second is having the knowledge that something needs to be accomplished, but the individual keeps procrastinating and putting it off to a later date.

To succeed, any good time management system needs to have two components at a minimum. The first is a task list and the second is a calendar. A third, often-missing component for real progress is the ability to set goals and focus on reaching those goals. The task list is critical to keep track of tasks as they arise and to have at your fingertips a method of capturing that information at the time it arises. The task list is also the tool you can use to make sure that you are making progress toward all of your goals every day. The calendar is critical to schedule and preserve blocks of time to complete the tasks that you have captured. Finally, setting goals and working toward them with persistence and breaking them down into manageable components is necessary if you are to make short-term and long-term progress toward reaching them.

When I first started practicing law, I was trained by our full-time private investigator/paralegal. He was a brilliant man. I am sorry to say he is no longer with us. His name was Vic Hedges. He taught me a lot. I will never forget what he said after I reviewed and triaged a large number of files after I was done. He said, "Now, Gary, forget about it! You need to clear your mind of all the details and attempting to keep them assembled for retrieval later. If you do that you will be distracted from the things you need to address in the moment. In addition, you will carry the stress of trying to remember everything with you. Don't do that. Once you have it documented and scheduled, forget about it!"

Forget about it! That's right, forget about it!

Manage Time to Be Able to Do What You Love to Do

You may have gotten through life without a good time management system, but you won't be able to succeed in practice without a system to keep track of all the details you need to manage as a solo business manager. In fact, you will not do well in any legal environment without a systematic approach to manage your workload and keep track of all the details. So you must learn to develop a system that allows you to retrieve information and control your workflow, or you will stress yourself unnecessarily and turn to drink or other unhealthy distractions.

My first legal job was as a public defender in a rural area in Michigan. I was assigned to defend clients who were charged with felonies. My first day on the job, I was told I would be responsible for nearly 200 active files. To keep track of all the details of those cases would have been an impossible task without a systematic approach. It wasn't like I could work a case from beginning to end, close it and move to the next file in sequence and put the old file away. Legal practice doesn't work that way. How, then, can you know of all the critical deadlines, and keep track of all the details of every case without dropping the ball?

When I was assigned responsibility for those 200 cases, I had to juggle multiple balls in the air at all times. This was a task that neither I, nor you, could do in our heads without losing sleep each night without worrying about whether you have taken care of all the things we needed to do. Would it be possible for me to keep pace with all the work and all the deadlines in all 200 cases? My mentor told me to triage all the cases, identify the tasks to be done, and create task lists and calendars to track all my activity. You will be faced with the same challenge; maybe you won't be faced with 200 files all at once. And initially, you may feel you can keep up. But as the workload builds and the pressures and demands of your business weigh in, you will find yourself overwhelmed and unable to cope with the pressures of tracking all the details of your legal practice.

As my mentor said after I documented each of my tasks, "Now, forget about it!," he made the point that you cannot clutter your mind with all the details of each case. You need to establish a system to allow you "to forget about it."

What follows are several rules that expand on what I described earlier, and I believe will help you sleep at night knowing that you have captured all of your tasks. It will also allow you to pace yourself and not miss deadlines. Do this for at least eight weeks and it should become a habit. But do it!

1. Get a system. You can use a paper or electronic system or some combination of the two. You can use your smartphone or tablet, but get out of the Post-It® Note mentality. Many systems are available for download on your computer, smartphone, or tablet. One that I was trained on and has helped me through my career is Franklin Covey™ management system (http://franklinplanner.fcorgp.com/store). One of the apps that I use is Planner Plus and it can be downloaded from https://itunes.apple.com/us/app/planner-plus/id560450229?mt=8 or at https://play.google.com/store/apps/details?id=com.appxy.plannerplus&hl=en for your Android. These have calendars, task lists, and the ability to

write comments. They are all portable and easily accessible. Google calendar also provides the user with the ability to list tasks and the tools to manage them.

2. Keep it with you always. This is important as it allows you to schedule an event, write down a task, or note important information you wish to retrieve later without relying on your memory to recall it later. Mark it down once and forget about it! If you memorialize the task as it is assigned, you will capture everything and not forget to log an item later. With smartphones, it is easier than ever to have, at your fingertips, the tool to record your task immediately. When you make a note of the task, then you can forget about it. As you read on, you will understand how you can be confident enough to forget about it.

3. Customize your system—personalize it so you will find the features well suited to your particular way of doing things. Make it yours and work to identify and implement all the features available to be efficient. Force yourself to use a system you really don't like and it will fall by the wayside from disuse. And you will find yourself missing appointments and deadlines. Keep trying systems until you find one you really like. Get a system that will synchronize across all of your information platforms so that you can rely upon what you capture.

4. Check it every day. This is your "tickler" system. Set aside twenty to thirty minutes each day to schedule your activities for that day. Make it a habit to do this at a set time, early morning or evening. Look at the calendar and your task list for the next day and the week ahead. Then schedule time to complete each task during the "soft" or "open" time periods. When others attempt to distract you or follow their agenda, unless it is urgent, tell them that you are scheduled for that time period. Offer to schedule a meeting with them during a time when you can give it your full attention and do a better job completing that task. "Pull the choke chain" and get their attention. Your time is important and distractions are wasteful time thieves. Don't be reactive—be proactive and use your time wisely. Checking it every day means that this is your tickler and those tasks you made note of earlier will be picked up and planned out on schedule. You can sleep at night with full confidence that nothing will be missed. (Turn off the notifications on your computer and cell phone for emails, texts, and the like. Do not look at them throughout the day as they will take you off task. Set aside times during the day when you check them en mass as opposed to constantly pulling away from your focused agenda. Getting back on track each time costs valuable time and wasted energy.)

5. Prioritize and moderate your tasks. Classify your tasks into three classifications;
   "A," critical—must complete today.
   "B," important—try to complete if possible.
   "C,"—complete as time allows.

This is a simple categorization. For another method that reflects the true value and urgency of a task, the website where the "Eisenhower Box" appears (http://jamesclear.com/eisenhower-box) shows a matrix and an explanation of how to distinguish "urgent" and "important" tasks from one another. An urgent task is one that is time sensitive and must be completed in a timely manner, whereas an important task is a task that requires your attention but may allow some flexibility in terms of time of completion. You can have tasks that are urgent, but not important. But if you have a task that is urgent and important, it will rank the highest in priority. The grid that you will find at that website demonstrates the difference.

What is important is seldom urgent and what is urgent is seldom important.

Dwight D. Eisenhower

Those that are urgent and important tend to get our attention first, but really those that are important but not urgent are the most important, because if they are not addressed, they will become urgent and important. The urgent and not important or not urgent and not important tasks are often the tasks that we give the greatest attention to and should be at the bottom of the list of tasks to be accomplished.

The problem that so many attorneys face is that they have failed to break their major tasks into smaller manageable chunks. For instance, if you are a criminal defense attorney and are assigned a murder case with a trial date looming in the not-too-distant future, it is easy to put that file at the corner of your desk where it will sit without any movement because it is such a large task to prepare for trial. The same is true for civil litigation or even transactional cases where there is significant work to be done.

The reason I see procrastination is that busy practitioners will look at those large files and think to themselves that they don't have time to get to those tasks today. The demands on their time are not small as there is a lot of work to do. If you are a law student, you might recall a paper that was due and that assignment remained in your backpack or on your desk waiting to be accomplished. Finally, when the pressure was too great and as the imminent deadline approached, you picked it up and it became a priority. You got it done, but it wasn't your best work product.

The solution is to break your larger tasks into smaller components. I suggest twenty- to thirty-minute tasks that can be accomplished without too much of an investment of your time. For instance, that murder case might be broken down into a discovery request for the prosecutor, interviews for each of the witnesses, or securing an expert for trial. Each of those tasks are discrete and may be accomplished fairly rapidly without setting aside an entire day or half-day to complete them. That way, each task can be annotated over many days so that you have competed all the necessary tasks before the trial date.

Chunk your tasks into twenty- to thirty-minute modules so that they can be completed without boredom or distractions setting in. Take that complex case and break it into chunks that are doable in short bursts. By having a system, you can pace yourself and spread the work out over many days and keep all of your case work moving forward.

If you use this system, you will never have a large file sitting on the corner of your desk gathering dust and finding yourself missing deadlines or being sued for malpractice. The side benefit is that you will be able to set aside time for your personal life as well. When you go to court, you will be prepared and not be counted among those attorneys who are constantly lectured by the judges for not being prepared for court.

Setting Goals

Follow these rules and you will be able to plan your life and set lifetime goals. Use those goals to identify twenty-year goals, annual goals, monthly goals, and daily goals, moving you incrementally forward in small steps—but making very real progress. Plan for your retirement and for your life after retirement with targeted time lines.

Attorneys who do this are the ones who come to court with just a few files. At counsel table next to them is the attorney who struggles every day trying to catch up. He comes to court with piles of files hoping he has in that pile what he needs to answer questions from the judge. In the meantime, the attorney (with good time management skills) only brings a thin file with what she needs in it. She is well prepared. As a result, she is able to answer the judge's questions before the disorganized attorney can find the information in his pile. The organized attorney has a reputation for being professional and prepared. Who do you think gets more favorable decisions when the judge can exercise her discretion? Need I say more? Follow these basic rules and you will find your life will still be busy, but your attention will be focused where you want to put it. Matters are not taking your life out of your hands.

Chapter 11

Grades Matter, but Your Success in Practice Will Not Be Measured by Your GPA

The good news is that if you did not do well in law school, that will not prove to be a barrier to your success as a practitioner. And, if you choose to go solo, you will not have to run the gauntlet of an employer's cross-examination regarding your grades or why you didn't attend a particular law school held in high regard by that employer.

Many WMU Cooley graduates find that employers do not fully appreciate the talents they bring to bear. This is largely because many of those potential employers have never attended their law school. The quality of education at WMU Cooley Law School, where I teach, is as good as you're going to find anywhere. Even though we don't have the highest ranking among law schools, this isn't reflected on the graduates' ability to practice law.

Because we have an open admissions policy, many individuals believe that the standards they have to meet to be admitted means that the quality of our students is not equivalent to those graduating from higher ranked law schools. It is easy to see why they feel that way as they compare the criteria for admission based on LSAT scores or undergraduate GPA. But in practice your LSAT score, school of origin, and GPA are rarely, if ever, known to your clients. And everyone has to pass the same Bar exam to be able to practice law in any event. Part of my task is to help my students understand that they have all the tools necessary to succeed in practice upon graduation regardless of which law school they came from or how they ranked in their class. Some of my readers will get it, however, many of them do not exprience that "awakening" until they get into the field and begin to practice law. Many practitioners undervalue their own skills. It is no surprise to me that they also fail to communicate that value to their clients when they graduated in the bottom half of their class. They were made to feel that that was indicative of failure by the higher performing students and their professors. This is reinforced further when they begin seeking employment and get rejection after rejection.

Think about it; if you didn't do well on exams, your GPA is not stellar. The good news is that it doesn't matter. . . . What I mean is that if you work for yourself, you will be the only one who matters. You will be the only one who knows what it was. More important, in practice, the law school exam is the polar opposite of the type of skills you will need to demonstrate in practice. To set an arbitrary time limit on the completion of a task, whether it is complete or not, is malpractice. To memorize the law and be limited to your memory without access to research materials when giving advice to a client is malpractice. To be denied the ability to collaborate with others is not the way it works in practice. I have found that many of my students, who did not do well on exams, were some of the best practitioners in our clinical programs. The reason for this is that they often understood best how difficult it was to grasp certain legal concepts. When it came time to explain them to their clients, their explanations were simplified and explored in a way that their clients could understand because those students understood how difficult it was to learn it themselves. As a result, they could empathize with their clients and relate to them better than some of the "higher ranked" students who might be frustrated by a client's inability to understand certain legal concepts.

This problem of a poor self-image is endemic at most law schools after the first year. And is grows even worse by the third year. The Socratic method employed in law schools is designed to reform your manner of thinking. But it has a cost. You are isolated and challenged before your peers by someone who knows how to make you squirm and be embarrassed. You are taught not to collaborate, as that would be cheating. So attempts to share what you know is inherently discouraged.

Why, if this is true, do so many employers look for the right law school on your resume and seek those students who have superior credentials? As a potential employer, you are looking out for the bottom line—profitability. Even if you are in a public service industry, you will still seek out those students who have the highest GPAs. Do you know why?

In some of the larger firms, status is conveyed on their advertising materials and school of origin; if it has recognition in their community, it will connect with certain clients. At least, that is one part of the equation. I can't change your school of origin, but I can make this irrelevant if you go into business for yourself.

The second part of the equation is class rank or GPA. The reason for so much emphasis on those factors has to do with profitability at the law firm. If

I hire someone who has done well academically, it is more likely that that person will be a quick study. That is, he should require less "hands on" oversight. For a partner, who is billing at $400 an hour, to spend time in the back room showing a new associate how to draft a motion or complaint at $150 per hour is very inefficient. Until you are productive, you are a "loss center" for the firm. They want you to become productive as soon as possible and to become a "profit center." They are betting that the student who has done exceptionally well in law school will get up to speed sooner than one who graduated in the middle or bottom of their class.

What you will find, once you enter the practice of law on your own, is that success isn't measured by your ability to "blind the judge with your brilliance." Rather, it will be measured by your ability to communicate effectively, play well with others, and to do the necessary background work to be prepared before going into court. For transactional work, you will find that preparation and organization again will be the key. But for both you will need to be able to communicate effectively and frequently with all of your clients and meet their expectations regarding timely and effective responses to their inquiries.

I've never practiced law as a solo practitioner myself. However, I come by the information I gather as a consequence of interviews that I've conducted over the past seventeen years with nearly every solo I have met. I also have engaged in a survey of nearly half of all the solo practitioners in Michigan to determine what it takes to succeed in solo practice. Finally, I have worked with students over the past seventeen years helping them to develop plans for their future careers; I periodically review these plans to keep them relevant. I stay in contact with them to assess my efforts and relative success in counseling them.

I have significant trial experience as a criminal defense attorney and more than twenty years of estate planning practice experience. I am in an academic environment where I supervise students as they prepare estate plans for live clients. But I continue to practice through them as I actively train students how to be effective counselors and practitioners. I have counseled students who come to me on a regular basis on how they might set up a successful solo practice. As a result of my exposure to the types of problems those students experience as they strike out on their own, I have created a series of programs to help them find their way to be effective and successful practitioners upon graduation, running their own solo practices.

Much of my time is spent undoing much of the emotional baggage inflicted on many of my students under the traditional law school training regimen. However, by the time I am done with them they are their own best advocates and fully appreciate the skills and knowledge that they can bring to bear to assist their clients. They also understand that there are so many resources, on the Internet, out there available to them that previously were unavailable. They can readily access those resources. They find that what they perceived as the most difficult task they are going to find in practicing law is not understanding the substantive law. Instead, it is the plan and path to their financial success. And that means they must learn how to "sell the sizzle and not the steak." This book will put you on the path to financial planning and success in the business of law. It is the one element missing from many practitioners' arsenal of tools. But in the end, your academic credentials will be far less important than your work ethic and willingness to constantly learn more about your craft. In law school you are led to believe that success in practice is going to be based upon the same skills necessary to blind the professor with your brilliance—not true in practice.

Chapter 12

Blinding the Judge with Your Brilliance: It Is All About Being Prepared

Railway? Stairway?

An old joke tells of two drunks walking the rails. One of them says, "Man, will these stairs ever end?" The other drunk says, "The stairs, I can handle, it is the railings that are killing me!" Perceptions . . .

You graduated at the top of your class. Congratulations!

Now let's see how well you do in practice. Because you were successful academically doesn't mean that you will succeed in practice. Nor, if you didn't do well academically, are you destined to fail in practice.

You graduated at the bottom of your class. Congratulations!

Some of the best students in my clinical program are not the ones with the highest GPAs. One of my students who graduated at the bottom of her class, was one of the best student lawyers I ever observed. How could that be? She knew the law. She just didn't perform well on timed exams. Also, she was able to break down concepts and simplify them for her clients in ways that some of the "A" students were unable to do because she understood the difficulty of understanding those legal concepts. She displayed empathy for her clients and took pains to be patient and explain those concepts until they understood them. Her clients, without exception, hugged her and made voluntary contributions to the clinic on her behalf.

If you think about it, law school exams are the polar opposite of practice principles. If an attorney relied solely upon their memory for the law and applied that knowledge to a client's facts while restricting the amount of time to come up with an answer; we might characterize that as malpractice. Students who don't perform well on exams don't necessarily perform poorly in practice.

But isn't demonstrated genius how you get jobs in "big law"?

GPAs are great sorting devices for law firms that sort resumes while seeking new associates. As the pile of resumes grows, it is imperative that the pile be reduced to a manageable level. Assumptions are made: hire someone with a high GPA and that will increase the odds that that person will be a quick study. They are more likely to be able to operate with minimal oversight.

You are a "loss center" until you can produce. The higher your GPA, the more likely you will be producing faster than someone who has demonstrated less skill in school at grasping legal concepts and demonstrating them on exams. The bad news for those of you at the bottom of your class is that it is becoming increasingly more difficult to find employment in law firms as many law firms reduced their staff during the downturn in the economy in 2006. As a result, there were more unemployed, experienced attorneys available in the pool of applicants. Mix in the higher performing students and if you didn't graduate at the top of your class, you found yourself taking jobs reviewing documents or other part-time work. This made it very difficult to compete for those jobs during that period. And some of the fallout of that period continues today.

But big law may not be your best job.

The good news is that if you put together a substantially viable business plan, and you pass the Bar, you have a job! And it can be a great job at that. What you will soon discover is that your class rank has nothing to do with your success as an attorney. Success in practice is not about blinding the judge with your brilliance. Rather, it is about being well organized and doing the hard work so that you are prepared when engaging others when representing your clients.

If you are willing to work harder than your competition, if you keep attuned to your clients' objectives and, finally, if you communicate consistently and effectively with your clients, you will have more business than you can handle. And not one of them will ever ask you where you ranked in your law school class. This I promise you.

Chapter 13

Lawyer? Attorney? What Is the Difference?

This chapter is not designed to help you establish your practice. However, it will give you background information that, amazingly, few lawyers/attorneys know. What is the difference between a "lawyer" and an "attorney" or is there a difference?

Years ago, a student in Georgia was clerking for a judge at an externship site. I was his supervisor. He told me that the judge would refer to lawyers and attorneys in a manner that seemed to imply that they were different. He didn't want to share his lack of understanding with that judge for something that was so basic. So he asked me if there was a difference. That sent me to the Internet to research the matter. Indeed, there is a difference, but not one that is widely understood or distinguished.

If you look at the definition of lawyer at http://www.britannica.com/EBchecked/topic/333070/lawyer, you will find the following: "Lawyer, one trained and licensed to prepare, manage, and either prosecute or defend a court action as an agent for another and who also gives advice on legal matters that may or may not require court action." Thus, a lawyer is someone authorized to practice law in a given jurisdiction under the rules for admission under that Bar.

An "attorney" comes from the French "atorné," or "(one) appointed." In other words, an agent for another. So "attorney" means nothing more than "agent." See http://www.etymonline.com/index.php?term=attorney&allowed_in_frame=0: "early 14c. (mid-13c. in Anglo-Latin), from Old French atorné '(one) appointed,' past participle of aturner 'to decree, assign, appoint,' from atorner (see attorn)." The legal Latin form attornare influenced the spelling in Anglo-French. The sense is of "one appointed to represent another's interests." Thus an "attorney" has a broader meaning than "lawyer"; it means "agent" in a general sense. This means that all lawyers are attorneys or agents, but not all attorneys (agents) are lawyers!

If you draft a power of attorney for your client, the agent is called an "attorney in fact." Literally, this means "agent in fact." Someone who is counseling clients and is a member of the Bar may advertise, "Attorney at Law" in recognition of their status as a legal practitioner and they are qualified to be an "Agent at Law" for individual clients.

So now you know the distinction, counselor. Next time the bar tab has not been paid, make a bet with your legal colleagues to see if they know the difference. I bet not.

What Area of Law Should I Practice?

As a law school professor for nearly twenty years, I frequently encounter students who say, "What area of law should I choose? How do I know what to concentrate in while in law school?" I tell them, unless they have prior experience in a specialized area of experience that easily translates into a practice concentration, they should not worry about it.

Ask any lawyer you meet about their current area of specialization and if they planned on that while in law school—from personal experience, I can say that the vast majority of them, over 90 percent, have told me that they didn't have a clue. So I tell many of those students, "enjoy the ride" and don't worry about it.

> *Worry is like a rocking chair, it gives you something to do, but won't get you anywhere.*

> Anonymous

Where I teach, students have little choice in their curriculum for the first two years. They must take evidence, tax, business organizations, wills, trusts, and estates, as well as many other classes, which they find to be difficult subject matter unlike electives that give them greater choice and usually are perceived to be less demanding subjects. However, those required classes are fundamental areas of practice and procedure. They lay the foundation and will give them the ability to take on whatever subject matter they choose to practice.

But even if you are not regimented and your law school "sets you free" to take electives after your first year, there are so many practice aids available. They are what I call "legal recipe books" for lawyers. Most areas of practice have them. They help you understand the A to Z for most areas of law along with practice tips. In law school, you are taught how to research and construct legal paradigms from scratch. But in the field lawyers employ those foundational skills only after tapping into work that has already been summarized and consolidated to increase their efficiency.

If it has been done before, they will seek it out or get it from someone who has done that work before. They then modify it with appropriate updates and changes. There is no need to reinvent the wheel when you are attempting to be efficient in practice. Almost everything has been done before. As a result, commercial resources and training aids are readily available online. Often, ironically, other solo practitioners are your best bet to get grounded in a particular area of practice. They are willing to share information, sources, forms, and tactical suggestions. This is not as true of attorneys in large firms. Solos own their time. They are in charge of their own timekeeping and not beholden to a partner to account for their time. The large firm lawyers are grinding out work on a set schedule based on the demands made of them by the partners. They don't have time left to "give away" advice to someone just starting out. And when business is slow, they are pressured to bill their clients to improve the bottom line of the firm, even though the associate may feel that those billing practices are borderline unethical.

As a result, today it is much easier to practice as an independent practitioner. This is due to available resources on the Internet and the ability to communicate with others through email from wherever you are with smartphones, tablets, and other linking devices in ways never envisioned even ten years ago.

Thus, I tell students to choose an area of practice that they can be passionate about. Be yourself and follow the path that allows you to grow as a person and one that you find interesting and enjoyable. As they say, "If you find something that you love to do, you will never work a day in your life."

> There comes a time when you ought to start doing what you want. Take a job that you love. You will jump out of bed in the morning. I think you are out of your mind if you keep taking jobs that you don't like because you think it will look good on your resume. Isn't that a little like saving up sex for your old age?
>
> Warren Buffett

Take a lesson from those who have struggled and learned to hate the law. Distinguish yourself from the rest of the lawyers in your area of practice or location. How do you do that? Watch what is going on around you! Over two years ago on my way in to teach a class, I was listening to National Public Radio as the host was interviewing someone concerning drones—not the big military versions, but the ones being used by hobbyists. As I listened, I thought, there it is—an opportunity for someone to recognize and act upon.

I entered my classroom of estate planning students and said, "drone law!" They looked at me like I was crazy. I went on to explain how the development and implementation of drones in daily life had legal implications that opened the door to lawyers for the provision of services to others concerning the use of drones and the legal implications of their use in business, municipalities, farming, criminal surveillance, and for private use.

I asked them to think about the current state of the law and how it might evolve. I offered all of them a gift—an idea and an opportunity. I told them, even two years ago, to write about drones and the potential impact and application of existing laws in their use. You can publish articles in law review journals, but those are highly specialized and not widely circulated. Even more important, they are not being read by the audience you may wish to reach. Consider writing copy that could be printed in a newspaper or online. Do that, and you will find that people will contact you for legal advice even while you are in law school. Advice which you cannot provide until you graduate and pass the Bar, but, you can refer those cases to someone who has passed the Bar and assist them under their credentials. You can become a "rainmaker" before you graduate.

Think about it: you are lounging by your swimming pool on a beautiful summer afternoon. Out of the corner of your eye, you spot something moving toward you overhead—it is a drone. You hear the high-pitched buzz of its propellers. In addition, as it is overhead you hear "click, click, click." You are not fully clothed! What are your rights to your image and the airspace overhead? Amazon revealed that they might be employing drones to make deliveries. Local law enforcement organizations are using them to search for missing persons and in drug enforcement. Recently, one landed on the White House lawn, and everyone went ballistic, concerned about terrorist threats using these drones, as they should be.

What is the state of the law? What legislative initiatives may be pending? What does the Federal Aviation Administration (FAA) have to say about drones and are there rules concerning their use for private purposes? Commercial purposes? Early in 2016, the FAA published regulations concerning the use of drones for private or commercial use. Recently, law firms have developed specialties dealing with drone law. Drones are just one of thousands of developments in technology.

There are also new cases decided in the courts, which have the potential for impacting consumers, businesses, nonprofit institutions, and governmental agencies. Every law that is passed is an opportunity to develop a practice in line with that development. The Affordable Care Act, 3D printers, same sex marriage, . . . the list is exhaustive. It is up to you to look about you and find what interests you and write about it.

Find an area of law that you are interested in that matches those things in your life that you are naturally interested in and make that your practice area. Try it out, start writing about that subject matter even before you graduate. Had my students taken up my suggestion two years ago and started writing about drones and the potential legal issues that they might pose in their operation, those students would now be getting calls from newspapers concerning current issues associated with the introduction of drones and applications that previously had not been on anyone's radar.

Keep your eyes open and look about you for opportunities in practice. If you are ahead of everyone and foresee the issues before they become popular, you will have little or no competition in practice. Supply and demand dictates that if you are the only one with a level of expertise, you can charge for that expertise. But be flexible and versatile. As a solo, you can "turn on a dime" with the advantage of decision making without having to consult with others and get their "buy in." This is a great advantage that you will have over firms with multiple lawyers. Committees are not the most facile entities to get things done quickly and efficiently. This means that if you see opportunities, you can probably take action long before their committees have met and agreed on a course of conduct going forward. Also, don't lock yourself in and refuse to reevaluate your position.

Chapter 15

On Second Thought, Not Such a Good Idea . . .

At this stage of your exploration to determine what type of law you will focus on, you need to be open minded and prepared to change course.

As you plan your business strategy, probably one of the most difficult decisions you may have to make is to change course. If you make a plan, give it time. If it doesn't work out, don't be afraid to backtrack—just don't burn your bridges. At times, we feel we have so much time and effort invested in a new process that we must go forward. Keep in mind, if you run the show, you are the one who gets to decide. Bury the baggage that you are inclined to carry, called inertia, and move on.

A True Story: "Just One Kiss Cathy?"

When I was in seventh grade, during the summer, Friday nights were special to me. I was allowed to stay out until dark because we didn't have school the next day. Often, I would play basketball on the playground hoops right near our house with friends. One Friday night, my friend, Claude, called me over to the grade school building adjacent to the basketball hoops to tell me that he saw some girls over at the school.

As a seventh grader, I was past the point of girls being a nuisance and began to see them as special and better than my male classmates. In fact, Claude and I would regularly cruise the neighborhood for "girlfriends." It was innocent enough. But hormones were awakening in us and we found the opposite sex to have some appeal. So when Claude alerted me to the fact that there were girls at the school, I was very curious as to what was going on.

Claude explained that he had encountered one of the girls standing outside the backdoor of the school. She didn't attend our school. She was there because her father was attending AA meetings on Friday nights at that location. She said she would be there on a regular basis. Claude introduced me to her, and an added bonus was that her friend also came with her father to the meetings. That meant there was one girl for each of us. Claude and I decided that I would adopt Cathy N. as my official "girlfriend" and he would get the other girl for his "girlfriend." From that point forward we could announce to the world that we had paired up and had "girlfriends."

We decided that we liked our new-found companions. But since their meetings went late into the night, we had to figure out how to justify staying out past dark so that we could spend more time with our girlfriends. In the end, we decided to tell our parents that we were offering to be altar boys for Novenas which was a Catholic ceremony conducted on Friday nights. Of course, we did no such thing. This excuse gave us cover to stay out late the nights when Cathy and her friend were at the school.

Our plan worked perfectly. In fact, for several weeks we met Cathy and her friend and found we enjoyed their presence. After about four meetings, Claude and I decided it was time to see if we could kiss them. We plotted and decided that the perfect venue would be the dark stairway leading up to the second story of the building where the classrooms were located. The meetings were held in the basement and lasted about an hour. We met as usual and instead of meeting them at the back door, we escorted them to the stairway and sat on the steps in the darkened stairwell.

All was going just the way we planned when suddenly Cathy's mom came around the corner and climbed the stairs in our direction. To this day, we don't know how she knew how to find us. Maybe by chance she was looking for Cathy and discovered us that way. In any event, she went into a rage asking us if we had any idea what we were doing. I can't imagine what she was thinking, but she was angry. She chased us out of there. In the process, she clearly told us that we were too young to be dating and not to approach these girls until we were old enough "to date and to drive." Believe me, that is an exact quote. With that, Claude and I decided that we needed to find new "girlfriends." Also, during our four weeks of meetings, we obtained their phone numbers and addresses. That was the last of our "Novenas."

Several years later, the day I turned sixteen, I got my license and already had a car. I had remembered Cathy and the statement that her mother made and decided that would be the day that I visited Cathy and took her mom up on her offer. On November 1, the day of my birthday, I drove to the north side of Fort Wayne to where Cathy lived. I knocked on the door and her mother answered the door. She didn't recognize me, so I told her who I was and recounted the story of our time at the grade school. I don't know if she really remembered me or saying what she said, but she yelled up the stairway to Cathy. Cathy answered and her mother told her there was a "very nice young man" there to see her. Cathy asked that I wait while she got dressed and after a few minutes she descended the stairway.

I didn't take Cathy on a date that day or any day. I didn't even take her for a root beer as her mother suggested. I couldn't get out of there fast enough! Cathy was not as I had remembered her. To be fair, it wasn't her appearance that bothered me, it was her demeanor. She "locked on" and wouldn't let go of my hand. She talked about going places and doing things together and dating. This was after her mother told her about how I recounted her statement that I was now old enough "to date and to drive" her places.

I made some excuse about having to leave. As I got into my car and departed, I thought about young love and how I had taken her mother up on her challenge and met it. This is not unlike challenges you undertake. You invest time and effort in processes that, in the end you find are not really working out. I couldn't wait to prove to Cathy's mom that I had more substance and persistence than she might imagine. My motivation to prove her mother wrong after my original encounter and scolding from her clouded my thinking.

We are often presented with new processes, changes, and methods, which others claim are going to make us much more efficient and which sound great. But the alleyways are littered with good intentions and software that never got fully implemented. First, don't grab for the first shiny object you encounter without doing your due diligence. Find more than one person who has tested the product or process, if at all possible. If you want to be creative regarding a new and novel area of practice, chances are that you will have a hard time finding others to give you feedback. In the end, you need to be honest. If you try something new and it just isn't a good match, it's time to change your strategy. You don't even need to find an excuse—just change your plan, but change it. Sometimes this can be very difficult to do. Once implemented we are often reluctant to give up a system (even a bad one) because we have to engage in more change, and we don't like change.

In the process I will set forth, you will be visiting other solo practitioners to find out how they have found their way. Keep an open mind concerning the area of practice you may wish to pursue, the population you wish to serve, and the processes that you plan to employ. Everyone you interview as you build your plan should offer insight into what worked for them and what didn't work. You will learn from those who are very successful and, in many ways, you will learn even more from those who operate on the fringes of success to see what held them back.

Homework

Come up with at least three different and novel approaches to the practice of law in an area currently not viewed as a legal specialty.

You can define it based on new disruptive technology (3D printers), or it can be based on a unique population (same sex couples), geographic proximity (areas of concentration where "fracking" occurs), or legislative initiatives (recent Supreme Court decisions).

Write an 800-word article about the development and how it might impact individuals, businesses, the legal profession, or governmental units. Find a publication that might find this topic to be of interest, and submit your draft for publication. If unsuccessful, try another forum in print, online, or even for your church group. But give it a try. Do not give legal advice until you pass the Bar. But general information, background, and prognostication is allowed. And have fun doing this. By the way, do this and you will have been "published" before graduation (put that on your resume).

Chapter 16

Rural Practice: Maybe You Should Look Outside the Crowded Legal Suppliers Market

Where have all the lawyers gone?

A student sought my advice recently about establishing a practice in a rural setting in an attempt to locate her practice in an area that was less saturated with lawyers. My advice to her was to concern herself less with the density of lawyers in a given area and more with a business plan that would succeed in the environment where she wished to start her practice. I tell students to first consider their values and set their goals consistent with those values. Those goals should set the stage for where you establish your practice.

For instance, if you value your heritage and close family contact, then establish your practice in proximity to your family and relatives. So when you start a family, or if you have established a family and went to law school later in life, you will have access to your loved ones so that grandparents and extended family can participate in your children's lives. As you age, you will often find that you are the caretakers for your parents. Of course, you can relocate your parents to your location, but it is far easier to keep them in place where they have established medical care providers and a network of established friends.

In the end, I don't feel you should select the location based on the density of lawyers as your primary consideration. Instead, I recommend you select your practice location based upon your values, ability to adapt, and long-term goals. In making your choice, however, you may find some diversity in the range of options available to you. And when considering those options, rural verses urban choices offer quite distinct advantages and disadvantages.

One of my graduates recently visited me from Fargo, North Dakota. He told me that he had a client who said he had to drive two hours to find a good family law attorney for his divorce. The client told my grad that he had to drive that far because there were no lawyers remaining in the town where he came from and it necessitated a two-hour drive to find a good lawyer. I have read about stories of rural areas and some urban areas where lawyers were aged and not being replaced or leaving those areas due to shifting demographics. As a result, a few are offering to pay off student debt if they move to those areas to establish their practices.

> Under Niagara Falls' plan, graduates who have earned a 2- or 4-year degree in the past two years can apply for up to $3,500 a year (for two years) towards repayment of their student loans. The same deal would be offered to graduate students. Graduates of Niagara University and Niagara County Community College will be targeted at first, though the city hopes eventually to recruit graduates from other parts of the country.[1]

In rural Kansas, a similar experiment is underway.

> Fifty counties in the state have established Rural Opportunity Zones (ROZs) authorized to offer one or both of the following financial incentives to new full-time residents: Kansas income tax waivers for up to five years and/or student loan repayments up to $15,000.
>
> To be eligible for loan repayments, applicants must hold an associate's, bachelor's or post-graduate degree; must have an outstanding student loan balance; and must establish residency in a ROZ county.[2]

To some, this may appear to be an attractive option. Indeed, they might choose to move to one of those areas. A recent issue of the *ABA Journal* was dedicated to rural practice options and that seems to be a popular topic in many blogs (now, including this one) as graduates look for employment options in a changing legal market. Certainly, this has appeal and I am not discouraging you from considering it.

In making your decision, there are other considerations at play. Recently, I heard someone say that there are some counties in Michigan where there isn't an attorney under sixty years of age. With an aging attorney population

---

1. http://abcnews.go.com/Business/towns-paying-off-student-loan-debts/story?id=16543649.
2. Ibid.

and shifting demographics, you may want to consider establishing a rural practice as your best option. However, unless you have connections in those communities and are willing to reach out beyond the local municipal or village boundaries to market your practice, you may find it difficult to secure a strong business presence.

The population of attorneys, like the population in general, is aging and has its share of "baby boomers" who are looking toward retirement. Every issue of the *Michigan Bar Journal* has a list, "In Memoriam" to recognize those members of the Bar who have passed away. Some months, that list is quite large and doesn't include those attorneys who retire and those who are unable to continue practice due to physical infirmities. Many of those senior lawyers are looking for someone to take over their practice. In some instances, this is an opportunity too good to pass up. But be careful. If I were to relocate to an unfamiliar area and purchase a practice, I would speak with one of the local court clerks to see how they react when you discuss the reputation of that attorney. The court clerks are often the first to hear about financial distress, grievances, malpractice, or attorneys who berate their subordinates.

Certain types of practices can be established with less concern with the location of that practice. Appellate practice is one example which would allow you to live anywhere you have good Internet access. If you want to do criminal practice in an area that is scarcely populated, you may find that you have to travel one or two hours a day to different circuits to maintain a viable practice based upon that area of law.

Many attorneys I interviewed said that you have to be a general practitioner in a rural area. I disagree. I know of a number of lawyers who run very successful specialized practices in rural areas. But they are very good at what they do; they are very well organized, and they aggressively market their practice beyond their local reach. Their clients are willing to travel or they are willing to travel to their clients.

If you think rural practice might be right for you, I would suggest you visit lawyers in that area to hear them out about the good, the bad, and the ugly of solo practice in that area. But don't be dissuaded just because a seasoned veteran says you can't make it. I truly believe you can make it almost anywhere. But try to discover as much as you can about the population, economy, and unique opportunities that geographic placement might afford you. Do your homework before making your move. And be discriminating and careful as there are so many options available to locate your practice with the flexibility that technology affords solos today.

Chapter 17

Card-Table Lawyer: Keeping Your Overhead Low

I once had a student gone solo contact me. He had just established his practice in a large city on the East Coast. He sent me pictures of his newly rented office. He bragged about the fine woodwork throughout and the full shelves of law books in the background. He looked almost "regal" as he sat behind the walnut desk and in front of the impressive bookshelves. When he called me to see if I saw the pictures, he assured me that "You need to look successful to succeed" in this city.

I told him that it looked very impressive, but cautioned him, as I had before graduating, to keep his overhead low. Chris was bound and determined to succeed and felt he knew better. He was motivated and he worked hard. However, as time passed, his correspondence grew more despondent. He explained that he got on the appointment list for criminal defense work and loved doing that work. He was successful at trial and enjoyed the action. But it was "low pay, slow pay." And it distracted him from developing a private pay practice. As a result, he was unable to keep up with his bills and even couldn't afford to get married. Finally, about a year after opening his practice, he closed his doors. He went to work in a small firm and gave up on his solo practice dream.

It isn't the environment where you work, that determines your success—it is about how you pay attention to the needs of your clients that fosters growth in your practice. You could operate from a card table in a broom closet and tell your new client—"I have never done this before, but I will tell you this—you are the most important person, and your problem has the highest priority on my list. NO ONE ELSE will give your issue the attention that I will. I may not have a lot of experience, but I know where to go to find the answers. I will give your case the attention it deserves."

First, be yourself and communicate your sincerity to your client and do your best. That is what builds a client base and ultimately, quality referrals.

Despite your best efforts, if you don't view your practice as a business enterprise and keep your expenses low while developing a profitable market plan, you are destined to fail. You may stumble through your legal career just staying ahead of the bill collectors, but that is not a marker of success. One of my former students, within three years of graduation, paid off her student debt and was debt free, with two offices and four employees. She has been very successful. But even more important, she has established business practices that preserve her quality of life while managing her practice. She even planned ahead so that she was able to take two months off to give birth to her new daughter. This year, she gave birth to another child and continues to expand her practice.

How? She left law school with a business plan. She was exceptionally resourceful, intelligent, personable, and stuck to her plan. She will tell you that she had no thought of going solo until we discussed it as a viable option in her third year of law school.

Many students ask me how much it will cost to start a solo practice. My answer—it depends! But in the final analysis, try to keep your expenses as low as possible; for every dollar saved is one less dollar that you will be able to keep for yourself. But make sure you have all the tools necessary and don't skimp on the essentials. Essential hardware and management tools should include:

- Malpractice insurance
- Laptop
- Scanner
- Copy machine
- Practice management software
- Smartphone
- Sequestered meeting environment
- Access to legal research resources
- Digital storage in the cloud or on site

If you have these essentials in place, you can operate from almost anywhere and keep your overhead to a minimum.

Malpractice Insurance

Malpractice insurance is essential. Fortunately, you don't start out with a book of clients so the insurer has very little risk. Some areas of practice have a higher likelihood of malpractice and insurance is priced accordingly. So you will need to check with your carrier to obtain specifics. Often, you can employ insurance brokers who will find the best rates for you. But don't "go naked" as they say. Take some of the worry out of your practice startup anxieties and get insurance for your piece of mind. Most claims arise as a consequence of poor communications with clients or missed deadlines due to poor time management skills (see Chapter 10 on time management to learn how to avoid those mistakes).

Laptop or Desktop?

If you can only purchase one computer when opening your practice, I would recommend a laptop. The problem with only one computer that is a desktop is the obvious—you can't take it with you. With the computing capacity in laptops these days, you can do everything on the laptop that you could only do on a desktop computer not that long ago. Starting out, and keeping your costs to a minimum, I would forego the desktop computer until you get better established. Even if you don't need the portability that much because you don't plan to leave your office that much, I would still go with a laptop so that, on those occasions when you have to leave for extended periods, like on vacation, you can take it with you. Even though I don't feel a desktop computer is necessary when you are first starting out, I would invest in a large flat-screen monitor so that you have the ability to work with multiple monitors open at the same time. Software is available to turn your laptop and flat-screen monitor into a repeater or primary source for a second monitor.

A check on the Internet for a few sources quickly identified the following options:

- http://www.maxivista.com/mac-as-a-second-monitor.htm uses a MAC as a second monitor for a PC by downloading companion software on both
- http://www.duetdisplay.com/ turns your iPad into a second monitor with a software download wirelessly
- http://www.pcworld.com/article/2089102/teach-your-laptop-to-treat-a-secondary-monitor-as-the-primary-display.html for more information on how to connect a second monitor to your laptop

If you invest in a laptop, make sure you get what you need. You don't need to buy a computer with tremendous video capacity required for gamers. Instead, you need reliability, good processing speed, and at a weight that you will find comfortable to use in transit. It may be possible to use the computer you acquired in law school, but make sure that it has sufficient operating systems for your practice needs.

As far as PC or MAC—either one is acceptable. But you will pay more for a Mac with equivalent capacity and there are more open source programs available for PCs than MACs. But if you are into MACs, like many users are, then by all means stay with a MAC. Many laptops have performance comparable to desktops and the portability of the latter strongly mitigates in favor of that platform when you are getting started. To give you specifics about which computer to buy would be a waste of my time and yours as the changes in operating systems, hardware, and other features will make my recommendations out of date even before this book goes to press. Instead, find an attorney you know who has up-to-date hardware and software. That is the person to ask about what information they used and sources for purchase that is consistent with the demands of your practice setting. Today it is highly recommended that you purchase extended warranty protection when purchasing a new computer as the useful life for most people is about three years. An extended protection policy can allow you to replace a computer that has failed quickly without leaving it for service. It should go without saying that continuous and rigorous backup systems are essential in the event of a breakdown so that you can retrieve your records without delay. As of this writing, you should be able to get a robust laptop computing system for about $1,500 to $1,800 and slightly more for an Apple product.

Scanner

Today, many courts require documents be filed electronically and that number grows every year. Accessibility of your documents from outside of your office is virtually impossible unless they are scanned and stored digitally. Scanners have improved to the point that you can do high-speed scanning with a high-quality scanner, which has optical character recognition (OCR) or "text searchable" capacity, meaning that once scanned, you can find anything previously scanned with search terms unique to that file, such as a client name, opposing counsel's name, phone number, file number, or any text unique to that file (e.g., "red 2008 Ford pickup"). Wherever that sequence of words appears, the documents will be sourced immediately. You can't do that with paper files.

Also, the cost of storage and maintenance of files is virtually eliminated. In the event of a natural disaster, you can store your files in the cloud and be backed up and ready to go without the loss of data. During Hurricane Katrina, many attorneys were put out of business or sorely handicapped as they scrambled to reconstruct their damaged paper files. The cost of paper, ink, and maintenance of sophisticated copy machines is largely minimized when you go paperless.

The scanner that I use, which is highly rated by most reviewers, can be found at http://scanners.fcpa.fujitsu.com. The company offers several models, some come with Adobe®10 read and write, which you can download to your computer. They can be purchased for about $400. The cost of that software is about as much as the scanner alone. These are versatile machines that will give you the freedom and independence that paper-based firms cannot exercise.

Data Storage Devices

If you are going paperless, then you will need to have storage and backup. If you are not going paperless, you are going to have to have storage and backup. This can be in the cloud, in a server in your office, or in a separate storage device. Most external hardware is now solid state digital and most have done away with disk or tape storage relied on in the past. Many can be encrypted. Most are available with terabytes of storage capacity which, at startup, should be more than adequate.

The most secure thumb drives, with levels of encryption that meet the highest level of federal government standards for security can be found at http://www.ironkey.com/en-US/encrypted-storage-drives/250-basic.html. Another option is Datalocker, with up to three terabytes of storage and self-destruct features like Ironkey, make this double authentication solid state device as secure as you are going to get for a portable storage device (http://www.originstorage.com/products/encrypted-solutions/datalocker-3/). But my personal favorite, as of this writing, is Cloudlocker at https://www.stoamigo.com/product/cloudlocker/. Cloudlocker offers features that allow you to store information on site in your office, in the hardware similar to the other devices. However, this one gives access to anyone you authorize without uploading it into the cloud. Sto Amigo has multiple patents which make this a very unique sharing device giving you access from any web-connected device. As the product's website explains:

> The CloudLocker is a personal cloud server that resides in your home or office and gives you complete control over all of your digital content via any of your portable devices.
>
> Simple to install, CloudLocker combines the capabilities of a leading cloud-based storage provider with the privacy and security of hosting your own cloud. By incorporating advanced sharing and privacy

features with "anywhere" access and control, CloudLocker delivers unparalleled power and versatility to the personal cloud marketplace.

And if you need more storage, no problem. Simply connect your own external hard drives to the built-in USB slots on the CloudLocker for unlimited storage expansion.

It also provides encryption capability that is on a par with your bank or credit union. I contacted the representatives from Sto Amigo to get updated information and they offered to send me a unit to test and I suggested they send a unit to one of my former students and current solos to get his impressions. I spoke to Chris who was testing it and he felt it was an excellent tool to use to share information with your clients securely and at reasonable cost. Since his practice was primarily criminal defense and family law, he felt transactional practices would be best served using this device—but it has potential for application across the board.

Digital Cloud Storage

When you first start out, you might want to consider storage in the cloud without local storage. You are already familiar with this concept if you use cloud storage like Google Drive, iDrive, Dropbox, or many others.

The following URL is a link to a site that lists ten cloud storage options that they outlined in 2012: http://www.cloudstoragebest.com/cloud-storage-types/. A more current site, updated in 2016, is http://www.cnet.com/how-to/onedrive-dropbox-google-drive-and-box-which-cloud-storage-service-is-right-for-you/. This site lists five of the more popular cloud storage sites with information about each of them.

None of these offer software as a service. Many cloud storage services geared to legal services will package the storage option with law office management software so that your computer is really nothing more than a repeater. You would be able to access everything from any computer, smartphone, or smart pad that your office produces. In addition, your clients would have the same access as you would authorize through your office "portal." I don't believe that when you open your practice you will likely need practice management software when you start up. But as your practice matures, you will likely need to consider it. With CloudLocker, or private servers located within your office, data is not stored in the cloud only accessed through a portal when connected through the Internet. If you are relying on the cloud as your storage device, and if the Internet is down, you will not have access to your data. Not true if you have an in-house server or use a device like the CloudLocker.

Printers

You will need a printer, even in a paperless environment as clients, administrative agencies, opposing counsel, and others will often require hard copies of documents. Invest in a good quality printer but you don't need to spend a bundle on this. Single-purpose machines are best, as you should have a stand-alone scanner and faxes can be done through your computer. So you don't need to buy multipurpose machines with scanning, faxing, and printing functions built into them. At first, you may want to keep your costs down by purchasing an inkjet printer for about $60 to $100. You don't need a color printer, but that is a feature of inkjet that you will get automatically that isn't standard with laser printers. Initially, the cartridges are cheaper.

But if you were to calculate the cost of the ink by the gallon, you will find it is in the thousands of dollars.[1]

If you have the means and want to invest in a laser printer, over the life of the machine, the cost of ink is what will be the long-term expense. For about $100 you can get a laser cartridge that will print as many as 12,000 pages and purchase a laser monochrome printer for as little as $60 with a starter cartridge installed that will get you through a few hundred pages of printing. And the quality of the laser printer for your own stationery will look more refined to the discriminating viewer.

Practice Management Software

The choices here are mind-boggling. You can get software for document assembly, file management, billing, time keeping, and integrated software for all of the above. I attend the ABA TechShow each year and many vendors come and go. Some are more stable than others. But they are all quick to tell you that you cannot operate without their system, and other products fall short of all the features that their package provides. The truth is that they all offer excellent features, but some are more comprehensive than others. Some offer better support than others. Some have pricing that is attractive today—but subject to price "enhancements." To switch over to another system later can be rather frustrating. I would recommend that you check with other attorneys in your local environment to see what they are using. Ask them how good the support, pricing, and long-term viability of their software has been.

---

1. See https://www.buzzfeed.com/higgypop/top-10-most-expensive-liquids-on-earth-6qcr for the "Top Ten Most Expensive Liquids on Earth." Black ink is listed at $2,700 per gallon.

Since they have no dog in the hunt, they will give you the best evaluation and recommendations. If you know someone else using the same software you have chosen, and you have a problem, often that user will be more attentive and responsive to your inquiries than a rep four states away on the telephone. For an excellent review of technological tools, hardware, software, and other devices, each year the ABA Law Practice Division publishes an annual guide that can be found at the following website: http://shop.americanbar.org/eBus/Store/ProductDetails.aspx?productId=268778331&sortby=Name+(A-Z)&perpage=36&ptopic=Law+Practice+Technology---Practice+Management~Law+Practice+Technology&page=2. This review is up to date and the reviewers are very candid in their assessments of devices and systems that are currently available. This publication is a good way for you to stay current and make informed decisions as you stay abreast of the latest technology.

Smartphone

I know of a few attorneys who still operate without smartphones, but they are becoming scarce. If you want flexibility and synchronization of all your applications and software—the smartphone is the way to go. Today, with voice recognition, Google Voice™, and many other applications, you can be connected and conduct much of your business from your phone. Look for battery life—there are phones on the market that will operate for two full days before charging is necessary. I know, I have one. There are so many apps that are available to make your life easier. Studies have shown that delays in logging time results in significant loss of billable income. Software can track time spent looking at emails, on the phone, and other matters seamlessly so that you don't miss out on valuable billable work spent on behalf of your clients.

Sequestered Meeting Environment

See Chapter 18, "Should I Work from My Home" for a discussion about that option. Notice, I didn't say "office space"? The reason I say this is that there is a trend toward "virtual office" meeting space. Today, attorneys work in "brick and mortar" offices, rent space on an hourly basis, and finally, many attorneys operate with nothing more than a post office box or mailing address depending on your jurisdiction's rules. How you choose to operate depends on your business plan, type of clients you will be serving, your area of specialization and finally, your budget. Today, because of the Internet and available operating systems, it is very easy to operate remotely from a physical office. As a result, many attorneys spend less and less time in their offices with some offering services sans physical office.

This can work very well depending on your area of practice. For instance, an attorney who does appellate work really doesn't meet clients in his or her office. Most of the research and writing and referrals are done over the Internet. In some instances, an appellate attorney can solicit work online, have the transcripts sent by email, draft an appellate brief, and submit it without ever meeting another human. Criminal defense attorneys often meet their clients at the courthouse, in the prisons or in jails, and never see those clients in their office. There are some attorneys who have "mobile" offices and meet clients who are homebound. Many attorneys meet clients in coffee shops, courthouses, or professional office buildings where conference rooms are rented on an hourly basis. Many of those services will accept mail or offer answering services as well.

One of my former enterprising students found an attorney with a large law firm who took a liking to him. They leased office space to him for evenings and weekends on a busy street very inexpensively. One evening that student called me to say, "Guess where I am? I am in the middle of a walnut paneled law library waiting for my client to arrive." The added advantage was that he was meeting with clients at times convenient for them. Eventually, he rented his own office; but contrast that attorney with the one who failed to understand how to keep his overhead low. While in law school, the graduate who I first described as unable to keep up with his bills, was always driving a new car and lived like a lawyer. The graduate who found an inexpensive setting to meet his clients, drove a very dilapidated car and dressed like he just came from a second-hand clothing store. Thrift was in his blood . . . and he is doing very well financially. Use some creativity and stay vigilant regarding your spending habits. But, at the same time, don't cut corners where you need to spend money to make money.

But, try to keep your overhead as low as possible.

Chapter 18

Should I Work from My Home?

If you have thoughts of working from your home, there are a number of considerations that I feel are important.

First, because your office is in your house, that means that you really will never leave "work." Psychologically, it can be a barrier to your ability to separate your personal life from your professional life. There needs to be clear delineation between your work environment and your personal environment or your family members, or even you may end up wandering into the work area if you are undisciplined and fail to separate your work life from your personal life. Clearly there will be times when the two will cross, but having an office in your home sets the stage for mixing the two inappropriately. You need to be able to get away from your work at times and having an office in your home will make that more difficult.

Second, do you want clients to meet you where you live? Most criminal defense attorneys would not want to invite individuals charged with crimes into their home. Thieves, child molesters, gang members, drug addicts, and so forth, are not the types of people that you might wish to invite into your home where your intimate living accommodations or other family members reside. What if you do only appellate work? In that case, you will not be dealing with clients in general and the client in your home issue may not be a problem. There is another problem of having clients in your home in that they may not respect your privacy and may view your office as open 24/7. Unlike a separate office, which you can close and lock the doors, your home is always going to be open in the eyes of your client. They may stop by and ask you a few questions, since they "happened to be in the area." This can become very annoying and troublesome. If you are a family law, criminal defense, or bankruptcy attorney, I would strongly counsel you against working from home.

Third, client perceptions may be influenced by your presence in your home. They might be less secure that you are established and going to be around for a while. Particularly, if you are just starting out, if they are aware that you are a newly sworn member of the Bar, or if you have a youthful appearance, not having a brick and mortar office may work against you. Further, having an office in a residential area versus in a commercial setting may undermine your credibility with some of your potential clients as well. Also, local zoning or reciprocal covenants for some housing developments may prohibit having or conducting business in your home.

So, if you find that you wish to establish an office in your home despite these admonitions, make sure that you have clearly delineated the workspace from the rest of your home. For IRS purposes, you will need to be able to do this anyway. Also, make sure that other members of your family respect that space as separate and distinct from your personal spaces and not to leave toys or other artifacts from the rest of your house in that area. For instance, it is not a good idea to have a sleeper sofa located in the office for overflow situations when friends or family visit. Remember, your client matters are confidential and if that person or others can have access to that information, you may be in violation of the rules of professional responsibility. So the office area and materials within need to be secured and inaccessible to others, including all of your family members.

Alternatives to Home Offices

Office suites or conference rooms are available in larger metropolitan areas for rent on an hourly, daily, or longer basis. You only pay for what you use and when you need it. This is one alternative to meeting clients in your home and preferable to meeting clients in a coffee shop or bookstore to conduct business. The coffee shop/bookstore venue may not afford clients the privacy they are entitled to and they may feel insecure about your enduring presence. It is better to rent a private suite for client meetings where you will have access to phones, copy machines, and limited reception services. The downside is that your name is not on the door and the client may feel less than secure that you will be around to serve them in the future. This may also limit the amount of referral business you might get from your clients. You may be able to charge lower fees under this arrangement, but in the end, that is not how I recommend you conduct your business with only saving costs in mind. Sometimes, you can save money at the expense of your business.

A True Story: The Salesman's Raincoat;
A Lesson About Management of Expenses

When I was a regional sales manager, the national sales manager was my trainer, and a very good one at that. On one occasion he told me the story about the salesman and the raincoat.

The salesman was on the road, visiting dealers out in the field on many occasions. During one visit, the salesman was meeting the dealer to demonstrate a piece of equipment out in the field and it happened to be raining that day. The salesman purchased a raincoat to be able to conduct his business and found it necessary to be present even during a rainstorm. The following week, he submitted his expense report and listed among his other expenses was "one raincoat."

When the expense report was returned to him with "one raincoat" crossed out and compensation denied, he asked the sales manager why? The sales manager said, "We don't authorize raincoats as a business expense." The salesman replied, "But, it was necessary for my business meeting and it is unlikely I will ever wear it again." The sales manager repeated, "It was not authorized and we will not reimburse you for the raincoat, end of story."

The following week the salesman submitted his expense report and again he listed the raincoat. And again the sales manager denied the expense. In the third week, again the salesman submitted his report and this time the raincoat was not on it. The sales manager saw the report and commented, "Well, I see you finally got the point. I see that the raincoat is not on the expense report this time." The salesman looked directly at the manager and said, "It's on there, you find it!"

The lesson my manager wanted to convey to me through this story is that I should not try to pad an expense account to increase my income. I had an unlimited expense account and since I traveled a lot, it would be easy to create receipts for things that were not necessary or real. He said that I should concentrate on increasing my income by increasing sales. He said all the time spent on padding expense accounts would be better diverted toward merchandising product and increasing commissions. He said I might make a little more using the expense account, but that that would pale in comparison with what I could earn by selling just a little more product.

For you, this is the lesson I want you to take away: don't try to "budget yourself into profitability." Instead, try to figure out creative ways to increase your business and the expenses will take care of themselves. This isn't to say I don't want you to be budget conscious. Quite the opposite. However, I want you to place even greater priority on EARNING MORE than on SPENDING LESS. Sometimes that means that you "take the plunge" like in the case of office space and rent a spot when you first start out. Even if you rent a space, there are ways to minimize the costs.

First, look for an office-sharing arrangement. But be careful with whom you associate! If you get into a group that has a bad reputation with the courts or the public, their "stink" will be your "stink." Do your homework and find out how they are perceived in the legal community. One way to determine their reputation is to ask other attorneys or judges. However, one of the best sources of insider information is to ask the court clerks how those attorneys are perceived. Then shop around. Very often a group of attorneys will have a room that can be converted to an office. No, it won't be a corner office with a window overlooking the urban landscape and impressing everyone who enters it. But for now you don't need to impress others with your work environment. Instead, you need to impress them with your motivation and desire to solve their problems better than anyone else. Your altitude is less important than your attitude. Where you make your case is less important than how you instill confidence and a following.

Now that you have found a group of attorneys with space to rent it is time to define the terms of the agreement. Many law offices have space that has been vacant for some time and they are willing to deal with you. See if you can get an income-based lease with a cap. That is, for the first month or two when you have virtually no income, you would not pay rent. After you start to generate fees, the rent would continue to rise and be capped at a certain amount. Offer to pay rent slightly above market under this scenario and rene-gotiate the lease at the end of one year. What is likely to happen is that you will be asked to cover hearings (offsetting some of your rent), doing research (offsetting some of your rent), writing letters or memos or conducting client meetings for other attorneys in your office, and the rent will become insignifi-cant. But be clear about what you are charging for your services to offset the rent and don't undersell yourself. Charge the market rate even though you are getting a rental offset.

The other advantage, and it is huge, is that your office mates will be avail-able to confer with concerning your cases. They will provide advice, forms, and send you business overflow that they will experience. Even though I highly recommend that you limit your practice areas and develop a niche or two, don't be afraid to try your wings and take on some new areas of practice during this formative period. Very often, attorneys find that a case that took them out of their comfort zone proved to be interesting and caused them to change their focus and develop a new and different strategy in their practice areas. The other advantage of an office-sharing arrangement is that most of the other attorneys in that office will be solo practitioners as well. Solos are not accountable to others for their billable hours and even though they might be busy, it is my experience that they are often more willing to give of their time than attorneys in large firm environments. Many of them will become great friends and mentors helping you to succeed.

In summary, consider working outside the home and think creatively how you might arrange your affairs to keep your costs low and your exposure and profitability high.

Chapter 19

You May Be Able to Earn More Than You Think as a Solo

In the article, "How Much Do Lawyers Working in Solo Practice Actually Earn?" by Michael Simkovic, written in July 2016 and posted in the Brian Leiter's Law Schools Reports blog, he cites an article by Professor Benjamin from 2015:

> In 2015, Professor Benjamin Barton of the University of Tennessee estimated for CNN.com, and Business Insider that attorneys working in solo practice earn an average of slightly less than $50,000 per year. Barton made similar estimates in his book, "Glass Half Full." Professor Stephen Diamond of Santa Clara argues that solo incomes are quite a bit higher.[1]

This observation was strongly disputed by Professor Barton in a subsequent email response and he gave his reasons why he believed the IRS data should be relied upon and that his assessment remains accurate and answered Mr. Simkovic in some detail in an attempt to essentially rebuke each of Mr. Simkovic's comments. As someone, perhaps with a "cup half full" perspective, who has been in contact with many of my graduates who have gone solo, I have to say that I lean more toward Mr. Simkovic's interpretation of the data than Professor Barton's; and as Professor Barton said, "Then I hope we can agree to disagree."

But, both Mr. Simkovic and Professor Stephen F. Diamon make the case that, in their opinion, a solo practitioner is probably earning, quoting Mr. Simkovic, closer to "$100,000" instead of the $50,000 figure quoted in Professor Barton's article. He comes to this conclusion based on a distinction between

---

1. http://leiterlawschool.typepad.com/leiter/2016/07/how-much-do-lawyers-working-in-solo-practice-actually-earn-michael-simkovic.html.

the IRS data set and Census data with the belief that the Census data is a more accurate depiction of earnings for solo practitioners. Frankly, you are in a class of one. Your only consideration is how much you earn, not what the average or mean is for your profession. But it helps to understand what can be demonstrated using statistical data so that you can look at averages and see what is projected as you prepare a business plan. You may be a class of "one" who makes $2 million as a solo or $100 in your first year. It makes no difference what others make from that perspective.

The IRS data, according to Simkovic, is flawed because the classification codes, which are used to identify categories of employees, includes quoting Professor Stephen Diamond's *Glass Half Full*:

> "Legal services"(NIACS code 5411) includes not only "Offices of Lawyers (NAICS code 54111)" but also *notaries* (NAICS code 54112), *title searchers*, and *other law related businesses* (NAICS codes 541191 and 541199) typically not staffed by lawyers and that are typically less lucrative than legal practice. The IRS has confirmed by email that its data includes these categories. However, the IRS does not have more granular information that would enable it to determine what fraction of "Legal Services" in its data constitutes "Offices of Lawyers."[2]

This would change the data to include lower earning individuals under the category of solo practitioners as Barton would argue. He also argues that in an attempt to show lower earnings to reduce "earned income taxes," many practitioners try to use every possible deduction available. As one who has a business background with independent business owners, I saw many of them take advantage of every tax avoidance option available, and they got very good at it. Some expenses that they were able to claim covered some expenses of living that a nonbusiness entity would not be able to deduct. I tend to agree with underestimating actual income. In contrast, the Census bureau data for "full-time self-employed, not incorporated" classifications would be more representative of true solo practitioners operating as sole proprietors as Barton described below.

> According to the U.S. Census Bureau's American Community Survey, average (mean) total personal income for lawyers who are "self employed, not incorporated" (a proxy for those in small legal

---

2. Michael Simkovic, "How Much Do Lawyers Working in Solo Practice Actually Earn?," July 26, 2016, http://leiterlawschool.typepad.com/leiter/2016/07/how-much-do-lawyers-working-in-solo-practice-actually-earn-michael-simkovic.html; emphasis added.

practice) was around $140,000 in 2012 and 2013. For those who were self-employed, incorporated (a proxy for those who are owners of larger legal practices) average total personal income was around $180,000 to $190,000. These average figures include those working part time. Restricting the sample to those working full-time increases average earnings for "self employed, not incorporated" lawyers to around $160,000 to $165,000 and for the "self-employed, incorporated" lawyers to $185,000 to $200,000.[3]

If correct, this would be a serious departure from the figures provided by Barton. Conversely, Barton, in his response to a post by Stephan Diamond, argues that Census information cannot be relied upon, in part, because it is reported anonymously. The numbers of solos that the IRS reports is more consistent with the IRS data than the Census number would indicate and that data from other sources further suggests the lower earning level. As of this writing, the conversation continues and, again, we can argue how many angels can dance on the head of a pin, but it really doesn't matter for you if you are attentive and have a good business plan that is well thought out and allows you to be competitive and cost effective.

What this discussion will do is open your eyes to the potential discrepancies that you are about to witness as you engage solo practitioners in your area in preparation of a sound business plan. My own experience with my graduates is that the first year earning potential is closer to $100,000 to $150,000 for those who possess the six characteristics of successful solos (discussed in Chapter 9). On the other hand, I know of others who struggle to earn $40,000 in their first year as gross revenues. For purposes of averages, if we take the low estimate that Barton suggests as accurate ($60,000) and add the amount that Simkovic suggests is representative of real average earnings of $100,000, and add the two and divide them, we get $80,000. This is still much better than "average (mean) earned income figures for all Americans reported by the U.S. Census's American Community Survey (around $47,000 including only those who are employed in some capacity, and $22,000 averaging in everyone—children, the retired, and those not in the work force)."[4]

Simkovic continues:

It seems likely that many small practitioners systematically underreport their net income on schedule C. Lawyers' sophistication and

---

3. Ibid.
4. Ibid.

familiarity with the legal system may suggest that lawyers are relatively well equipped to reduce their tax bills legally, for example by claiming deductions. In 2013 IRS average business receipts for legal services sole proprietorships was around $116,000. Deductions and exclusions averaged around $67,000. There were 70,000 returns for sole proprietors in legal services with no net income that still generated an aggregate of $1.6 billion in revenue. To the extent that claimed deductions or exclusions really reflect personal consumption or clever tax planning, business receipts may provide a better guide to true income than taxable net income.[5]

Simkovic also points out a fallacy in data collection and reporting that I have often referred to as producing an inaccurate picture of solo practice income and employment. He explains that income reporting early in establishing a solo practice is like any business development. Early earnings are going to be very low as you will be investing in building the business and it takes time to get it up and running. But you will be building equity and value that stays with you. What is that worth? Who do you have to rely on for continuation of your employment? What is that worth? There is no value attributed to the ability to operate independently and make decisions without the approval of others before you can make changes. What is that worth?

Also, once established many solo practices run on "auto mode." What I mean by that is most of the mature, established solos will tell my students that their marketing is virtually all "word of mouth." That is, they can rely on repeat business based on prior contacts or referrals from former clients and that they are no longer doing aggressive marketing. They have systems developed and in place that allow them to have much greater freedom and ability to conduct business with most of the learning curve behind them.

Finally, Simkovic concludes that in reaching his conclusions, Barton misses the mark:

> Differences across data sources highlight the importance of apples-to-apples comparisons within a single data source and context. Unfortunately, Barton mixed and matched different data sources, comparing low estimates from IRS data for legal services sole proprietorships to higher estimates from other sources for workers other than lawyers.
>
> Comparing across sole proprietorship categories using only the (flawed) IRS schedule C data shows that legal services ranks near the

---

5. Ibid.

top of industries based on average net-income. In 2013, Legal services trailed offices of doctors, dentists, and securities brokers, but was well ahead of sole proprietorships in most other industries, which accounted for more than 97 percent of sole proprietorships. This ranking matches Census and BLS earnings data, which shows lawyers typically trailing doctors, but leading most other occupations.

In other words, lawyers remain among the highest paid occupations and legal services appear to be among the most profitable small businesses.[6]

Bottom line, I feel that data can be wrong and that most of the "seers" out there have gotten it wrong and that you can do better financially than their prognostications would seem to indicate. The more important question is, How well can YOU do with the tools that you have at your disposal? A well planned strategy to establish yourself as a successful business entity is not the product of how well or poorly OTHERS DO. That has no bearing on your success or failure. You can do better than others if you have the work ethic, plan, and execute on that plan—then your income is unlimited. I have seen it so many times before. You are only limited by you!

What will it take for you to be successful? Read on.

---

6. Ibid.

Chapter 20

How to Get More Out of Law School

I set out early on to help my students understand with greater clarity, some of the opportunities for self-employment. From my own experience with students who graduated from a lower tier law school, it occurred to me that many of my students would end up in practice for themselves or in small firm settings, but they did it by default, not with a plan. Most of them were unprepared for the reality of the practice of law as a business venture. They couldn't afford to delay earning an income, to establish themselves and begin to earn a good income. Law students need tools and guidance. That is what I set out to provide them with and I have done so for almost twenty years.

In a study by Robert Half Legal® in 2016 a question was posed to "350 lawyers among the largest law firms and companies in the United States and Canada." The question posed was, "What, if anything, do you wish you had learned in law school that would have better prepared you to practice law?"

The responses were telling. To me, they were not a surprise. As you read this book and about my background teaching in a law school designed to prepare law students to be practice ready, these are the essential principles I live by and promote among all of my students, regardless of their ultimate placement as solos or in law firms. Their top responses:

1. More legal knowledge/skills—33%
2. Business knowledge/skills—32%
3. Personal/soft skills—23%

These were the top responses among those who are employed in some of the largest law firms in the United States and Canada. I will briefly describe below how you can improve your status before graduation so that you are better prepared for the real world of practice after graduation.

More Legal Knowledge and Skills

The legal knowledge/skills component is one which, as a clinical professor, I find to be easy to understand. Until my students represent their first client, they are truly ignorant of process. Sure, they understand substantive legal principles, but not "as applied." You can only get that through the application of those principles in real life. That is when the "light bulbs" go off. The first time you meet with a real live client, you will have to explain legal concepts to the satisfaction of your client. You will need to understand those concepts adequately to translate them from "legal gibberish" to concepts that the client can understand. That is when it will hit you—it is not about getting a grade any longer, it is about hitting the target by exploring that information to the satisfaction of that client. And that client will be totally different from your last client, who will be different from all your other clients. Each message must be uniquely tailored to each individual. How successful you are at doing that will dictate whether your client base grows or not.

So, what baffles me is why every student in law school doesn't participate in a live client clinic if one is available to them. Think about it—you get to practice law *before you graduate*! What could be a better learning experience? The reason knowledge/skills is at the top of the list in this survey (and probably at the top of the list of most lawyers), is that only upon graduation and being thrown into the practice environment that the realization that you really don't know what you are doing until you do it. So why wait until you graduate to employ those skills? The other advantage of doing it while in law school is that you practice at the risk of another person's law license! So, my first recommendation is that, if at all possible, enroll in a live-client clinic as soon and as often as you possibly can if it is offered at your law school. That way you can get the "knowledge and skills" that legal professionals (like those in this survey) say they wish they got more of while in law school. You won't be a "well-oiled legal machine," but you will be way ahead of your peers who did not do so.

Greater Business Knowledge/Skills

While in law school, the business of law is not emphasized. This is particularly true in the first year or two of law school before you have had a chance to take electives. The required courses focus on doctrinal law and the fundamentals of legal theory. If your law school offers an elective geared toward the formation and management of your law firm, it is probably limited in scope and duration. Some of the more progressive law schools will devote more electives to this subject matter. Where I teach, we offer a number of electives; Accounting for Lawyers, Entrepreneurship for Lawyers, Transition to Legal Practice and, of course, Law Practice Management. In addition, I offer a directed study which has as its final assignment, creation of a business plan geared to the geographic location and area of practice that the students wish to focus on. Those business plans are based on each student's independent observations and based upon information they gleaned from attorneys in those areas to determine how they might structure a practice to be successful. In my opinion, every student should engage in the preparation of a business plan before graduation using that process. It is "transformational" in the words of a number of my former students. This is the foundation that you can build for your legal career and will set you apart from your peers. It will force you to look ahead realistically and set goals for yourself. All the work you do is for you and has real potential to help you become successful in whatever area of practice that you choose. (More on this in Part II of this book.)

Personal/Soft Skills

What are these skills? They are the interpersonal skills that most people learn as they are being socialized. Some are what I commonly call the "Carnegie" skills, named after Dale Carnegie's 1936 publication, "How to Win Friends and Influence People." These skills combine to allow the ability to connect with others and foster good feelings and confidence in your ability to get the job done. These skills really cannot be taught. However, they can be enhanced by participation in groups like "Toastmasters," to learn to speak more effectively and convincingly. They are the verbal and nonverbal messages that we transmit with awareness and some that we engage in unwittingly; both good and bad messaging. Some of it is social skills or awareness. We have all met someone who interrupts the conversations of others without prompting and at inappropriate times. We know individuals who talk too loud, too close by invading our "space." Some of these skills can be enhanced through coaching, but many of them are so ingrained and part of our personality that we will find them difficult to change.

Also, for every characteristic I find offensive, you might find someone who is not bothered by it at all and, in fact, feels it is a good quality. What I find outside of my norm, another person might find to be within their sphere of acceptable behavior. There are some actions, however, that are not acceptable anywhere at any time. For instance, swearing at others with no apparent realization that they are offending anyone.

These social skills are what often make the difference between being offered a job and being rejected. First, you have to be aware that you do or do not possess these skills, or someone may have to tell you. The problem is that the very person who needs to hear that message, because of their lack of social skills, may not be able or willing to hear it from someone else.

These three skills—the ability to connect with others, foster good feelings, and possess confidence in your ability to get the job done—are some of the important factors for you to consider as you make your plans. If you have properly prepared or if you are willing to make adjustments to gain those skills, then you may be ready to start on the path to preparation for practice. I have tried, over the past twenty or so years, to help my students and other individuals referred to me to find the path to their success. Below, I briefly outline some of my efforts. Keep in mind, I see this as a "work in progress" and will continue to modify my approach, even as I research and write this book.

Chapter 21

How Do I Find/Make My First Job?

Although the focus of this book is on how you might establish yourself in business as a solo practitioner, it is very possible that after reading this book and conducting interviews, you might decide to seek employment with another. So this chapter will offer some suggestions if that is your approach and ultimate outcome.

If you recently graduated and have had difficulty getting responses to your resume and cover letter, don't be discouraged. Many attorneys won't bother to respond to resumes and cover letters sent "To Whom It May Concern" (TWIMC) because, frankly, it won't concern anyone. . . .

For students seeking references from me and asking me to forward it TWIMC, I refuse to send it because it is a waste of time for them and for me.

I'm a great believer in luck, and I find the harder I work, the more I have of it.

Thomas Jefferson

Create a Business Plan

Follow the recommendations I make in this book to prepare a business plan for the area of law that interests you. Interview local attorneys and find out what they say about areas of opportunity and how they have established their own practices. What have they done well, and think about what you would do differently. Ask them to tell you about the good, the bad, and the ugly of going solo. Create a viable business plan for you to go solo as a backup plan. Put it in your back pocket when you engage in interviews for jobs later on. When that firm makes an offer that you think is unreasonable or embarrassingly low, reach into your back pocket, pull out your business plan and thank the interviewer for the opportunity to meet them and decline the offer. That business plan will change your approach and you will no longer appear to be "needy" and in desperate need of a job. You already know that you can make what you are being offered by going it alone. The best employer you will ever have is YOU, remember that. Also, after reading this book and putting into practice some of the concepts I have described, you will be thinking like a business person. You will consider profit centers and revenue streams, balance sheets, and assets and liabilities. When you interview another for employment, hopefully, you will frame your inquiries in the context of a business arrangement with a potential employer and have greater appeal for that employer as a result.

Go to Court

If you are new to the area and if you do not have local connections, go to the local courts and meet with court clerks. Dress well, but don't overdress. Bring copies of your resume and wait until they are not busy. Explain that you are going to be working in the area and want to work for someone who treats others well and has a good reputation with the courts.

After engaging them, when you feel you are connecting with them, and you will know when that is happening, it is time to ask to leave a couple copies of your resume with them. When they give you eye contact and really seem interested in you, that is the time to strike. Be honest. Tell them that you need the work. But try not to appear desperate. If at all possible, find out something about them and be genuinely interested and find out what you can about their background. After all, you will be working with them on a regular basis in the future. Make them your friends.

As they talk, look for parallels with your own life. It could be schools, friends, hobbies, or any of their interests. The minute you find common points of interest or connections, you become more familiar and connected to them, and more closely associated with that person than others. The tone of the conversation will change and that person becomes your friend in a way they were not before you made the linkage. That is what LinkedIn is all about, establishing professional relationships based on common acquaintances or professional interests.

There is no substitute for interpersonal contact. When you seek a service, are you willing to contact someone "in the blind" without looking for reviews or references? Probably not. And now, with the Internet, many attorneys will use LinkedIn or listservs to post openings and seek new associates from other attorneys who know the candidates and will recommend that person based upon their interactions with that person.

Many ads seek someone with one-to-three years' experience. You are not in that category if you are a recent grad. Hopefully, you participated in a clinical program in law school to gain practice experience. The supervisor of that program is the best reference you could get, because they can speak to your ability to engage live clients in a meaningful way and that supervisor has observed you in a controlled environment and can gauge your abilities.

Finally, if you want to find a job, remember: it is all numbers. The greater number of contacts you make, the greater the likelihood that you will make a connection to link you to someone who will help you get your first job. Every dead-end you experience puts you one step closer to a positive connection. But sending resumes out in large numbers will be a disappointing experience. You are better off spending the time reaching out and networking.

Be Out There Where Attorneys Gather

Attend local Bar meetings. Bring resumes just in case someone is willing to take one to forward to someone else. If you find that people offer to assist you, get their business card, take them up on their offer, and send them a thank you card, if they spend time sharing their knowledge with you. Do not send an email. It will be deleted before it is even recognized.

Volunteer at legal aid. But they will need to get a commitment from you concerning days and times that you will be available. Be consistent and fulfill your commitment. What will impress them the most is that you are a person of your word and that will be very important as opportunities arise. Remember: half the formula for success is just showing up. Employers are not looking for grads who will "blind the judges with their brilliance." They are looking for workhorses who have staying power and the ability to get along with others. They are looking for individuals who demonstrate a good work ethic. Your volunteer work becomes a working interview, which builds your frame of reference working with the courts and with clients. Do not sit at home transmitting copies of your resumes to people you do not know. You are better off getting out where attorneys gather and connect with them whenever you can.

Go to court and sit in on hearings during "motion day" for each of the courts. The judges will ask you who you are and why you are there. Tell them that you are a new attorney in the area and trying to learn how to be effective for your clients. Tell him or her that you are looking for a job in the area and if the opportunity arises, ask the judge if you can leave a resume with him or her.

While attorneys are waiting for the docket to be called and are sitting in the hallways, it will give you an opportunity to strike up a conversation about why you are there and what you are seeking to accomplish. Don't push for a job with anyone. Simply explain what you are seeking and leave it at that. Again, if the opportunity presents itself and you feel that you have connected with specific lawyers, ask if they would be interested in having a copy of your resume in the event they hear of an opening somewhere. Get their cards and send thank you cards to everyone you met who gave you five minutes of their time or shared useful information with you. As you engage in conversations with those people, make sure you do most of the listening and less of the talking. Remember the 25/75 rule. You should do 25 percent of the talking and they should do 75 percent of the talking. Ask them about themselves and keep on asking until they have painted a clear picture of what is important in their lives. Be sincerely interested. Take notes for later use to refresh yourself about those you meet so you can recall those details later. Keep doing this and if you do it right, job interviews will start to appear.

Finally, consider writing about a topic that is of interest to you in a local publication, bar journal, or on the Internet. What is currently in the news and how does the law apply? How might consumers, attorneys, courts, or businesses be affected concerning recent changes in the law? Be creative and first to address those implications. Writing general information pieces in 500 words or less can go a long way to help you get attention from potential employers or potential clients. Even if you haven't passed the Bar, that doesn't mean you can't write about legal topics. You can't give legal advice until you pass the Bar, but until then you can explore the potential implications of a new law. If someone contacts you concerning their specific concerns, you can refer potential clients to other attorneys with their consent. What would be a better point of reference than your ability to generate potential business? Send a couple referrals to another attorney and you will be viewed as a "rainmaker" even before you have passed the Bar.

Whatever you do, don't waste your time waiting for someone to call you. Get out there and become actively engaged. Make that your full-time job until you get the offer you seek. Good luck!

Part II

Get on Track to Start Your Own Practice

Chapter 22

Exploring Your Possible Options, Putting Everything in Context, and Understanding the Rudiments of the Legal Profession

This book was designed to guide you through a planning process.

In an attempt to make this book as useful as possible, I have organized it in a manner that is designed to progress from the standpoint of someone who has decided to go to law school and wishes to have a plan in place at the time of graduation to establish himself in the legal community. At the conclusion of this book and during the planning process, the journey you embark upon many not result in the outcome you anticipated. In fact, I would be quite surprised if your perspective hasn't changed. The primary focus and guidance takes you toward development of a solo practice as I find that this perspective will be helpful to you whether you end up in solo practice or end up working for someone else in private practice or as an attorney in a nonprofit or as in-house counsel for a corporate entity.

One of my goals is to provide you with a framework that allows you to find your way to success in practice on your own or working for others. The process that follows will expand your sphere of influence and help you establish relationships with attorneys and court personnel where you will eventually practice law. You will develop an understanding of how various practice regimens take advantage of your natural strengths. You are also going to identify other practice models, which may not play to your strengths. Another outcome may be that you decide that solo practice is not your best option.

Even if you decide not to go solo, all of your hard work will not be in vain. Many of the students who have undertaken this process get job offers from the attorneys they interview. The reason is that as they engage attorneys to find out how to be successful in business, those attorneys are very often impressed with that approach. It signals an understanding of how the practice of law really works and tells them that you are likely to be successful. Often they will share your enthusiasm and ask if you would consider joining their firm.

Can you build a business plan to go solo and still seek employment from another after graduation? Of course you can. In fact, having a viable alternative—your "back pocket plan"—will allow you to interview for employment without feeling needy or desperate. You do not have to take whatever comes along. You can be more discriminating and selective.

Finally, as one of my well-respected colleagues from a large firm background once said, "Even in a large firm, you are a solo nowadays or you will not survive." If you do the groundwork you will be more productive in a large office culture since you will have a better understanding of how to market yourself and gain efficiencies in practice.

Chapter 23

A Recommended Timeline to Put You on the Path to Success

This process can and should begin during your first year of law school. Your first task is to succeed in law school. During the first year you ought to investigate multiple types of legal practices so that you can better understand what various types of practice look like. A student will say, "I really like criminal law" after completing a first-year class in criminal law and doing well on the exam. They might like the classroom experience, but that is very different from the practice of criminal law as a defense attorney or prosecutor within the legal system. It is important that you investigate various specialties to find out how they work in practice. During your first year, your task should be to better understand how various types of practices actually work in the field. This will help you narrow down your areas of interest later on as you define the areas of practice that you will plan for in the future. You will also do the preliminary research to help you establish the geographic areas of interest where you might want to establish your practice. Much of the research has already been done at the state Bar level. Frequently, you will find surveys of that state's lawyer population with results concerning the number of attorneys in counties or parishes. It will often give you fees charged based on the size of the firm or the range of experience. Demographic data will give you information regarding the size, age, ethnicity, income status, and so forth of a given population. Look at it in assessing where you want to establish your practice and where there might be a greater need for the services you will specialize in providing.

You will also be engaged in creative ways to minimize your student debt through part-time employment that enhances your understanding of practice principles later. Find housing that reduces your student debt by working out deals with local residents to share housing with a senior or other person with fixed or limited income who is looking for a roommate at a cost that is below market in your area.

During your second year, if you follow the sequence I recommend, you will venture into the field to establish contacts and network with professionals in the area where you wish to establish your practice. You will continue to investigate areas of practice that offer the greatest potential in that area. As you establish relationships with other attorneys, bar associations, para professionals, and businesses you will begin to make connections and see what is the best fit for you, your personal values, and your desired lifestyle. As you do, you will draw a clearer picture of the local legal culture and see how you might fit in. As you begin to develop areas of law that interest you, you may begin to write about those subjects and find ways to get published.

During your third year, you will be sent out to conduct interviews with other attorneys and spend time questioning them to see what they are doing well and not so well. From those interviews and your research of current trends and practice management systems as well as current technology, you will begin to prepare a detailed business plan that you will use upon graduation to establish yourself in solo practice. You will continue to publish materials relating to your core area of interest and establish yourself as the "go to person" for your established area of interest even before you arrive in the community.

Upon graduation, you will, first, be engaged in committing yourself to dedicated and focused study to pass the Bar. Without your admission to the Bar, you will not be able to maximize your revenue stream and establish your independent business. During the period after you have taken the Bar and are waiting for results, if you follow my guidance in this book, you will be engaged in work to set the stage for opening your practice after being sworn in.

Once the doors are open, it will be time to monitor your progress using metrics that give you a clear understanding of whether you are on course to meeting your goals or if adjustments are necessary. You will need to continue to "feed and water" your plan and constantly be on alert to update and make adjustments to stay on course and remain competitive.

Chapter 24

Understanding Your Best Options. Start Early: Build Your Practice While Still in Law School

Start by Learning the Lay of the Land

I have created a course of study designed to help students in their third year to prepare a viable business plan before graduation. During your first two years, you will have conducted a survey of different areas of practice to better understand what it would be like, day to day, actually practicing in your areas of interest. To my knowledge, my program is unique among law school educators. Frankly most of the work is being done by the students. I coach them and guide them through the process, but they execute the plan. I share resources I have gathered over the last twenty years. They are materials that practitioners have been using to improve their efficiency and ultimately their "bottom line." Students use those materials to learn how others are finding success in solo practice. Then they try to integrate some of those innovative and established processes into their business strategies. Students are sent into the field to meet with practitioners in the geographic area where they plan to set up their solo practice. I instruct them to find solo practitioners who are the same gender and same ethnic background as the students. That way, the students will more clearly define the challenges and opportunities that they will encounter when they start their practices.

Each student must interview at least four solo practitioners in the area where he or she plans to practice. Finally, one practitioner interviewed must have over ten years' experience, one less than three years' experience, and two more with any range of experience. The seasoned practitioner will have a substantially different approach to marketing, technology, and practice management from the new startup. The new startup will likely be familiar with current technology and software resources, and will be more likely to approach marketing using social media and other resources that may be unfamiliar to the established practitioner.

The three-year solo will be dealing with student debt and entry into the market with a significantly different population of attorneys than what the seasoned veteran experienced when he or she entered practice. The seasoned solo will rely more on "word of mouth" for marketing and be well connected with the community. He will probably still be keeping thick paper files stored in file cabinets throughout their office. By visiting a range of practice models, students are better prepared to understand the vagaries of practice in the area where they intend to practice. These interviews serve to allow them to connect with and establish relationships with some of the more prominent members of the Bar where they will practice. In addition to four solos, each student must visit at least one judge and one court clerk.

Students are told to introduce themselves and use these interviews as an opportunity to LISTEN MORE AND TALK LESS. They have a series of open-ended questions to use during the interviews, but they are instructed to allow the interview to go in whatever direction the principal wishes to take it. (See **Tips and Tricks for Effective Interviews With Established Practitioners at the end of this book.**)

Solos are solos for a reason, and most of them want to remain independent. Most of those attorneys are not interested in hiring an associate, although there are exceptions, which will be explored in later chapters. If they sense someone is trying to get a job with them, they will put those students off or decline to meet with them. I tell them to explain, up front, that they are not seeking a job and that they want to work for themselves. In addition, they are instructed to dress business casual so the attorneys they interview don't feel like it is really an interview in disguise. Students have considerable background material at their disposal, which they review before engaging in those interviews. When they interview those solo attorneys, judges, and clerks, the questions that they ask are pointed and informed. As they conduct those interviews they have an understanding of how to uncover or discover the information they will need to be successful.

At times, students in rural areas find that the number of available attorneys is limited, so they expand their area of investigation beyond their local area. They are not limited to solo practitioners if they feel there are other attorneys in small or large firm practices who are willing to meet with them. The purpose of focusing on solos, which are of the same ethnic background and gender, if at all possible, is to give those students a clearer picture of the type of challenges that they will experience.

During this process, those students meet with me in groups of five to discuss their findings and to share their experiences with the other students in the group. As this conversation expands and continues for seven weeks, sharing what they learned with one another offers guidance and insight into the implications and considerations the other students might want to incorporate into their business plans. This gives all the students greater exposure to the problems and opportunities real lawyers in the field are confronting. By sharing in this manner, they all become more informed of the current issues in practice management.

Finally, they prepare business plans specifically tailored to their individual needs, challenges, and unique characteristics. Those plans become templates for execution after graduation. Many students, who have engaged in this process, describe it as "transformational." Many of the business plans that they submit are very creative and grounded in the realities of their market and often incorporate ideas shared by others within the group. I really encourage collaboration and tell them I am only interested in a viable final product.

A few of the students who have undertaken this process have decided not to go solo. Some have chosen to establish a practice in an office-sharing arrangement with other students in their group. Quite a few of their interviews have resulted in job offers from the attorneys they interviewed. I have yet to have a student take them up on a job offer, but I have had a couple enter into an office-sharing arrangement with some of those attorneys. One attorney even offered to fund one of my student's new office as a partner in that new venture. The student declined that offer as well. Once the students begin to see the opportunities before them, they usually want to go it alone.

For the business plan, I give them the following instructions:

Summarize all the visits that you made and identify several particulars concerning those practices. At a minimum: Where are those practices located? How long has the solo been in practice? How long as a solo? What kind of office is utilized? Comment on software, marketing strategy, billing practices, area(s) of practice, and employees, if any, being utilized.

Tell me what you learned for each visit that was beneficial and helpful and moved you forward in your planning. Also, point out what you learned NOT TO DO from that visit. Finally, tell me of anything that really surprised you from that visit that you never expected to discover.

- What are they doing well?
- What can they do better, incorporating materials we review with specific recommendations?
- How will this improve their bottom line or efficiency?
- What will you adopt from their practice and how will you do so?

What impact has this review made upon your decision to go solo? Have you decided against going solo at this time and why?

In the body of your plan, I want you to include the following in whatever order you feel works best.

- How have your feelings changed concerning the decision to go solo? Stronger? Weaker? Unchanged?
- Discuss the following:
  - What area or areas of law do you wish to pursue? Why?
  - Where do you plan to establish your practice? Why?
  - Whom will you rely on to mentor you? Or do you need to establish that relationship as yet?
  - What are the unique strengths that you will bring to this area as a solo practitioner?
  - What is your greatest weakness in pursuit and establishment of your solo practice?
  - When do you plan to establish your practice?
  - How will you finance your practice?
  - What are your startup expenses and first year budget?
- Explore how you will set up your practice concerning your:
  - Computer system
  - Software or practice management systems
  - Docket storage—cloud-based or in-house server, or some combination of the two
  - Research access
  - Printer
  - Scanner
  - Malpractice insurance
  - Office or sequestered environment, virtual practice
  - Furnishings
  - Advertising method and budget
  - Phone system
  - Health insurance
  - Bar dues

- How will you be organized: Sole Proprietor/PLLC/Partnership?
- What social networking will you use, if any?
- What web presence will you have?
- What professional organizations do you plan to join?
- Finally, how will you distinguish yourself from other attorneys in your area? In your practice specialty? In your ability to communicate? In your personal connections? And how will you stay abreast of developments in the law and business in general to stay fresh and competitive?

Chapter 25

Get Out There During Your First Year in Law School

Go to Court to Mix and Mingle

During your first year of law school you need to do what most law students fail to do—go to court. That's right; go to court. You don't need an escort, you don't need permission, you won't get a grade for doing this. Then why should you do it?

Students will spend three years in law school and rarely, if ever, go to court during law school. This is truly amazing when you think about it. It is a profession they have chosen to practice, presumably, for the rest of their lives and they lack the curiosity to see how it works in practice. Because they are not directed to do something, they don't see the value in doing it.

Why would I direct you to go to court? To see judges and attorneys interacting. To see the underclothes of your mistress—Lady Justice. For watching the justice system in action is often like making sausage—not real pretty but the outcome can be quite beautiful if you fully understand what is going on. Sometimes the outcome can be abominable as well. You will get a flavor of what it is like to actually practice in an environment that is designed to move the docket and where justice is not the ultimate outcome.

You will also get to see the quality of representation, both good and bad. This is your chance to see those attorneys who the judges and other members of the Bar respect and those who are always running late, come in unprepared, and represent clients who are hard to control. What is the difference between those attorneys who are held in high regard and those who are not? Is it demonstrating a brilliant intellect? Do they stand before the judge and blind her with their brilliance? I think not. No, the good ones, if you look close, are the ones who are prepared, know their cases, and are able to access information as the judge requests it. They are the ones with good working relationships with the court clerks, judge's secretaries, and other court staff. They treat everyone, right down to the janitor, with respect and dignity and most of all, they do the hard work and preparation before coming to court.

One major difference between the two is that the good ones have a good time management system. The inept attorneys are constantly arriving late and bringing large stacks of files with them to court because they are not sure where the relevant documents are located. And opposing counsel is prepared and answering questions before the poorly organized attorneys can locate the information sought by the judge. When the judge has discretion when rendering an opinion or ruling on a motion, who do you think has the advantage?

Go to court on "motion day" when the courts have the greatest numbers of cases scheduled on the docket. Visit the courts of general jurisdiction that can try cases in equity and in law. Visit the lower courts where the amounts in controversy are small and where landlord-tenant cases are heard. Visit as many different courts as possible and visit often. Very often the judges may ask who you are and why you are in court. Be polite and tell the judge that you are trying to learn how the law works in reality as you try to find out what you want to do upon graduation.

Between hearings, many of the attorneys will be waiting to be called and may be seated in the court or halls. If you have a chance, sit near them and wait for opportunities to speak with them concerning the matters that bring them to court. Ask them how they ended up in their area of practice and about the opportunities and difficulties of practicing in that area of law. Learn everything you can about various specialties. Ask how many different areas of practice that they engage in and how they feel about future prospects for those areas of practice in the future. If they offer to do more and allow it, you might see if you can "ride along" for a day to see what it is like to have a family law, bankruptcy, or estate planning practice. You are not a threat as a student and you are not looking for a job, so many attorneys will share some of their wisdom with you if you just ask. Learn to talk to attorneys; you will be doing it the rest of your life.

Define Your Brand and Find Those Who Can Help You Get the Word Out

In Chapter 15, you were given "homework" to find and define an area of practice that is new to the law. After you define it, think about how you might establish a brand using that as a way to define your unique skills and abilities to address this new and, hopefully, evolving area of law. Let's say you got published and found a niche that you wish to pursue. Take it to the next level. And, yes, you can do all of this while you are still in law school.

One Great Tip: Find the Influencers!

If you want to expand your brand's presence and work smart, you might be wise to consider information shared at http://relevance.com/this-social-media-illusion-can-help-you-boost-your-brands-presence. The post by Lillian Podlog describes a study done at the University of Southern California, which identified and explored the "majority illusion" and how that concept might be used to increase your business. It really is nothing more than finding individuals who, as I call them, are more importantly connected.

For example, say you are marketing widgets. You tell your close friend about your American-made widgets. Your friend is impressed with your widgets. He tells his twenty friends about those widgets. They are impressed with your products; however, this does nothing to enhance your sales or business profile as none of them are ever likely to purchase your widgets.

What if you provided the same information about your widgets to someone who is connected with a circle of friends who are associated with an organization called, "Widgets Made in America"?

In the first example, your business wasn't advanced. Your friend may have been an "influencer," but the people he influenced were not the category of individuals who would ultimately influence those who might be potential customers. Sure, you impressed more people with your wonderful widgets, but it did nothing to grow your business. In the second example, your friend was an "influencer" connected to your ultimate audience. He had the very real potential of connecting you to those who might purchase your product or raise your profile among a special group of people. He expanded your influence among those who might be interested and who might purchase your product.

In the estate planning realm, this might be akin to telling a friend who is a pet owner that you do pet trusts. This might result in one new estate planning client. You expanded your business by one transaction. Alternatively, what if you had contacted a pet supply store manager and told her that you do pet trusts? You might tell her it is an area of specialization that you emphasize and a special service you offer for all of your clients. You may have spent the same amount of time communicating the same information to two different people with very different results. The pet supply store manager has a reach well beyond herself and would have the potential to connect to multiple consumers of your service. Take that to the next level and seek out those in that industry who are well connected to other pet store operators and in a position to share your expertise to those individuals and your web of connections expands beyond the retail level to other wholesalers. If your services are designed to give clients planning features that are unique and distinguishable from your competition who also do pet trusts, then you have the potential to gain even greater access to your target market.

This strategy goes hand-in-hand with Chapter 34, "Wholesale Versus Retail." However, the emphasis in this chapter is on whom you target based on their ability to influence clients who seek your services even more dramatically. Leverage your efforts to their greatest potential and you will realize greater returns given the amount of effort you expend.

Target your market like a laser and use your time efficiently by targeting those who are most likely to reach those you most want to reach with your message. Think about those individuals who are strategically connected AND have the power and ability to influence those you know are potential clients. Spend more time planning your approach and you can spend even less time getting your message across with even better results.

Homework

Identify the Influencers in your life. Contact at least three of them and tell them about your desire to develop greater understanding and expertise in subject matter that they are involved with. Seek their guidance in developing your specialized area of practice and ask them to weigh in on your idea. Use them to critique your approach. Use them to expand on your ideas and to use their experience to help you better understand the issues that may arise in the context of developments in the law.

Chapter 26

Continue Your Investigation and Interviews with Local Attorneys

You are now in your third year of law school and looking forward to graduation. If you have made it this far, it is highly unlikely that you won't finish and end up with your JD. In Chapter 23, I provided the outline of a plan for you to go into the field to research your options and start to make connections while in your second year of law school.

As I explained, that outline closely follows a program I have in place to formally guide students through the process of creating a business plan. That plan begins with supplementing those students with marketing and technical information, giving them a better understanding of how lawyers are being coached to enhance their profitability and productivity. Then they are sent into the field to interview lawyers where they intend to practice. Finally, after interviewing those attorneys for the good, the bad, and the ugly of going solo, they prepare a business plan. That process is necessary to understand how lawyers succeed and how they fail. In the process, you get to prepare a business plan cultivated and nurtured with the tools and operations that will set the stage for your own success.

If you followed recommendations made in Chapter 6, you have already engaged attorneys in your community to better understand what you will need to do to be successful in your practice. In this exercise, I am asking you to expand your area of influence and understanding beyond the local area where you plan to practice. I want you to do a regional examination and investigation. Look statewide. You can do this by contacting Bar Associations in your state and asking for leaders in the area of practice that you anticipate making as the mainstay of your practice. Ask them about establishing a practice and what they feel is important to know. What you will be doing is making contacts with individuals who have a statewide reputation who have figured out how to be leaders in that area of practice. How did they establish themselves and what would they recommend for someone just starting out? I will venture a guess that they are active members of a section of the Bar with a leadership position. You are likely to find that they have narrowed their area of specialization. Remember: LISTEN MORE AND TALK LESS as you conduct those interviews. And don't forget to send a handwritten card of thanks, not an email, but a real card with a stamp and words of gratitude for taking valuable time out of their busy schedule to help you.

Also, in this second round of exploration, continue to meet with as many solos in your area as you can and continue to interview them to discover what you will need to know to understand the market and local practice opportunities.

If you have not already met with your school's financial aid personnel, take a trip to that office and see what options you might have to defer your student loans and manage your student debt in anticipation of a period of low earnings until you get on your feet.

You are encouraged to use a series of open-ended questions during the interviews, and allow the interview to go in whatever direction the person you are interviewing wishes to take it.

See if there are other graduates from your law school who will be seeking employment or setting up practice in your area and form a support group. Get a list of alums from your law school who are established in that area and use that as a list of contacts to use as possible people to interview.

Finally, update your business plan to reflect what you have learned from your latest research and interviews.

Chapter 27

Write, Write, Write

You need to write—before you graduate, after you graduate, during your practice. Even if writing was not your favorite subject in law school, it is your means of making a living. You will need to be a competent and persuasive writer to be successful as a lawyer so you might as well practice until you can do it well.

While in law school, you had to produce writing that was properly researched and footnoted. Maybe you wrote for law review at your school with very strict formatting requirements.

Now, as a lawyer, much of your writing will not be for submission as an appellate brief. Rather, much of your writing will be "lawyer letters" making a demand for payment on behalf of your clients, or correspondence to clients or others on their behalf as their representative. Much of the writing that you will do will be persuasive and semiformal. But much of it will be mundane and related to subject matter that you develop as your area of expertise. In time, you will develop your own file of letters and a form bank with letters that you will reuse over and over again. Those are letters that you will refine and modify only slightly as needed.

I would like to encourage you to write about something that really excites you and gets your blood flowing while still in law school. It may be law related, but it need not be. The idea is to develop a writing style that promotes your hobby, passion, or your sense of adventure. It might even be fiction. But any writing that you do will hone your skills and make you a better legal writer. It will help you to be a more persuasive writer in your legal writing.

Ideally, if you practice your craft for something that you are passionate about, you will carry over those traits to your legal writing. In writing a brief, it is writing to your audience (the judge) and knowing your judge will help you win your legal battles. Recently, I heard of an attorney who drafted an amicus brief entirely in cartoons. The judge instructed the parties to the lawsuit to keep the briefs to a minimal number of pages. This lawyer engaged someone he knew who was an amateur artist, and the judge was someone the attorney knew quite well. (I wouldn't try this on someone you don't know.) I saw it and it was pretty amazing. As they say, "a picture is worth a thousand words," and it was apparent that that attorney made his point in a very clear and concise manner.

Follow the news and write about current events and how they might be impacted by the law or vice versa. Pick your topic based upon what you find interesting. Even if it isn't a specific legal topic, it can be unrelated. But if you get published and have your name in print, it means that more people will be reminded that you are out there and when they have a legal issue, it is more likely that they will think of you if you are fresh in their mind from an article that you wrote.

In Chapter 14 I suggested topics that you might consider, including drones and 3-D printers. Look at the news and current decisions in the courts that have the potential to affect individuals' liberty, property, or relationships with others. How might business be affected by new legislation passed or proposed? How might this topic tie into what naturally interests you? If you find you are connected, you will be a more effective writer and have a better understanding of how things might affect others.

So, in between those times when the phone isn't ringing or the doorway is empty, pull out your laptop or tablet and begin to outline an article. Keep it short, under 1,000 words, and think about local papers, or papers that focus on certain groups or topics. Finally, start a blog and keep posting material on it to keep it fresh and in demand with ideas about how the law may affect individuals in their daily lives. Be out there; write about what interests you and others will be interested too.

Chapter 28

Prepare to Pass the Bar Exam

This should be your full-time job right after graduation.

If you have finally obtained your JD, now is not the time to relax and celebrate. Some students who have done well academically have decided to do minimum study or to forego a Bar prep course altogether. Some students have told me that they couldn't afford a Bar prep course and took the Bar in hopes that they might pass. Other students have engaged in full-time employment after law school to help pay off their debt, and that is commendable. However, if your employment doesn't allow you to focus on preparing to pass the Bar, you will be making a big mistake. Now is not the time to place other priorities before studying and preparation to pass the Bar exam.

You have invested three years and thousands of dollars in your law school education, now you need to make sure that that investment will pay off with a license to practice that profession. When studying for the Bar, use a commercially prepared and up-to-date system. When I studied for the Bar exam, I treated it as a full-time job arriving at a library with a friend of mine. We arrived at 8 a.m. and quit at 5 p.m. Every fifty minutes, we took a break for ten minutes and then went back to work. We did that because without those breaks, you will get fatigued and be unable to absorb what you are reading. Test yourself as often as possible, as learning theory suggests that it is the retrieval of that information that forms synaptic connections much better than study without retrieval.

We continued that process every day except Sunday to give ourselves a rest and to break the monotony of study. We both passed on the first try. Thus, I suggest an approach that is disciplined and complete. If you do that, you will find it gives you greater confidence when taking the exam and, I am convinced, you will be more likely to pass on your first attempt.

What if you do your best in preparation following a strict routine but you do not pass the exam? Well, the truth is that many before you have failed the exam and it is no measure of your ability to succeed in the practice of law. Put it behind you and start over and take it again and again until you pass. If you take the position that you want to wait another year or put some time between your last attempt and a new attempt, you will be putting greater distance between a period of continuous law school study habits and the new exam. The greater that distance, the more chance that your retention of that material will be lost. So stay the course and keep trying. With each new attempt, if you fail, you are just one test closer to passing.

Part III

Marketing: Your Biggest Challenge, Your Greatest Opportunity

Chapter 29

Sell the Sizzle, Not the Steak: Part I

Marketing 101

Understand that what you feel is important in your practice doesn't matter to your clients unless it is defined by what your client's needs are.

Telling others that you are an estate planning attorney tells them nothing about how you might serve their needs.

Alternatively, if you examine your possible audience concerning their potential needs, you might come up with a different way to define your practice so that you address what they perceive to be problems that they have or unaddressed needs that you identify.

I recently met with a former student who had gone out on her own in practice. She opened her doors several months ago and has restricted her practice to estate planning and family law. Her plan is to further define her area of practice as she continues to build her client base. She told me that she enjoyed practicing family law and asked me how she could reach more of those clients.

I told her to define herself to deal with a need that is not being met by looking about her and finding a new and evolving area of practice not yet defined. We discussed the possibility of engaging in a practice that specialized in collaborative resolutions. This is a new and evolving type of family law practice that attorneys have tried to promote. It meets the need of those who are looking for dissolution of their marriage with the least amount of emotional capital being spent.

Those practitioners define themselves as standing out from the rest and practicing family law in a nontraditional and nonadversarial family law practice. They promote themselves as attorneys who maintain harmony, as much as possible, within the family unit. That is their sizzle.

There are family law practitioners who serve segments of the population based on the gender of their clients. Some offer specialization in representation of men only in divorce proceedings. They explain that they understand the special considerations of representation of men and why men need to understand why judges may treat them unfairly. They promote themselves as experts in representation that focuses on possible prejudice of the judiciary in those proceedings toward the men in divorce proceedings. They fulfill the expectations of those men who feel they might require greater sensitivity to their needs as a man, which is the sizzle that those family law attorneys sell.

For the graduate I met, I suggested she look about her for sizzle that no one appears to be addressing. In 2015 the U.S. Supreme Court came down with a decision *Obergefell v. Hodges*, which determined that there is a fundamental right to marry that is guaranteed to all, including same sex couples. Given that decision, we now have same sex couples who can be legally married in all fifty states. Who out there is specializing in same sex couple divorces? Up to now, there have been many couples who have lived together without legal sanction of those relationships. What will happen now that they can get legally united in marriage in the event they want to get a divorce?

The sizzle for those couples would be in some respects the same as opposite sex couples when divorce is imminent. However, the sizzle will be quite different because of their unique relationship as a same sex couple. For instance, if they are two females, traditional roles and strategies may not unfold as in the past. One of the partners may be the dominant partner and one subservient. Because of those roles, a practice could concentrate on the special needs of the caregiver for children they may have together. Instead of representing men, a practice might concentrate on representing dominant or subservient partners based on the characteristics of each of the partners in that relationship.

For now, how do the laws address divorce in the context of same sex couples? Many of the laws have not been written to address that form of marriage. For instance, in Michigan the legislature in Michigan eliminated dower. Dower is a right that the female in a marriage has as a consequence of her marital status solely based on her gender. Males are not entitled to dower. With the recent decision by the U.S. Supreme Court, it is generally understood that the law will be revised to eliminate dower altogether. But the implications raised by gender-specific laws under the *Obergefell* decision will mean that family law attorneys will have to sort it out as those laws and legal relationships are newly interpreted in light of changes in the law. I told my former student to do what I tell all my students—"write about it." But look for potential problems under the current statutes and suggest how those laws might change. Are there any cases being litigated under the latest decision from the Supreme Court? What kind of issues are being litigated and with what result? Tell your audience about that and feel free to suggest how other courts or jurisdictions might adjudicate those conflicts. Suggest changes in current statutes that might address issues that are bound to arise in the context of those conflicts. Write short, well-documented, and authoritative articles in the publications (paper or digital) that your potential audience is likely to read. Or go for general populations in newspapers of general circulation and get the word out that you specialize.

And with changes in the law, what issues might arise for same sex couples? What issues might arise that have not been envisioned by most family law attorneys? Be the first, and be the best, in representing individuals and defining your sizzle in such a way that others are not competing against you. Do this and you will stand alone and clients will seek your services as you are not only an expert, you are the only one who sees the problems that will arise in the context of their conflict. Your pricing is the by-product of the special skills that you bring to bear as demonstrated by the fact that you were interested enough to write about it. Your pricing will not be generic, nor will it be aligned with the fees charged by every other family law attorney in your area. You are different as you meet their special needs.

Most attorneys focus on their practice area and forget to see that they are nothing more than a solution to their clients' special needs. As a result, the practice of law has evolved to serve individuals' general needs and has failed to adapt to the changing norms. Because of disruptive technology, we have seen the values associated with the practice of law diminish in many individuals' eyes. People can go on the Internet and read about legal principles. Often they try to educate themselves when they need legal advice by reading legal websites. They often believe they can substitute good legal counsel with Google searches. What follows is a short story about how there is no substitute or shortcut for good legal advice. They are often unable to foresee the "parade of horrors" that lawyers envision who are trained and experienced in the practice of law.

A True Story

Years ago I was employed by a veterinarian during high school to work on weekends cleaning cages that were used to board animals. On the weekend, I would feed and give water to all the animals and put them into runs so that they could exercise before returning them to their cages. Every weekend, almost like clockwork, a couple would bring in a dog in a padded basket to the clinic to board him for the weekend. This dog was a German Shepherd and the reason that he was in a basket was that he could not walk. He was paralyzed. I had to carry him out into the dog run and lay him on a pad while I cleaned his cage, and often had to clean him after he soiled himself. I changed his water and gave him fresh food. He would lay on his side and dip his head into the water and food dishes as he could move his neck. But he could not move the rest of his body. I felt so sorry for that dog. I wondered why someone would be so cruel as to keep him alive in that condition.

The vet explained the reason this dog was kept alive. While the dog was still healthy and the owner was alive, the owner established a trust on behalf of that dog to care for him as long as he was alive after the owner died. The owner loved her dog and took the steps necessary to make sure that the dog was cared for after the owner died. However, the owner had not anticipated the fact that the dog would suffer a stroke and be kept alive under the circumstances that had developed.

I tell my students that they must ask if their clients own pets and determine what their goals are in fostering the care and comfort of those animals upon their death, or in the event of those animals' disability. Most students who take this class are concerned about the *things* clients own and how they will be distributed at death when drafting their wills.

When the students ask if their clients have any pets, those clients often tell stories about their dogs, cats, birds, and other pets. When asked what would happen to those animals if the client were to be killed in an auto accident tomorrow, they look stunned. My students soon make the connection with their own concerns about animals that they own. As they hear the story about the dog in the basket, they often talk about their own pets and the fact that they never thought about who would take responsibility for their care.

As one who has practiced law for many years, if a client came in seeking an estate plan, each session would involve an in-depth conversation about any animals that he or she owns. We would address the goals and establish a care plan for those pets. Many of our senior clients ask that their pets be euthanized. This is particularly true for older animals that may not be able to adapt to a totally new environment. They wish to avoid an outcome where their pet might be mistreated or abandoned.

To avoid the problem that the "dog in the basket" above illustrated, it would be wise to establish a trust for any and all pets' benefit. In addition, one should identify a custodian to care for the client's pet and that person could be the successor trustee. However, as someone experienced in estate planning,

I would recommend setting up a "trust protector," which Michigan law allows. The trust protector would be able to change the terms of the trust, terminate the trust, change the custodian, or take other steps to prevent unintended consequences. But the most important part of this arrangement would be that the trust protector be given the authority, at any time, to authorize or direct termination of the trust in the event that animal's welfare was no longer being served. In addition, the trustee would be authorized to euthanize the animal or to make other arrangements concerning the care and custody of that animal. That way the custodian could be paid a monthly maintenance fee, but the animal would not be kept alive simply to keep the payments coming.

*It is important to understand that you are providing a valuable service in the counsel that you provide. It is not the paper product generated that is the valued component of your service; it is the counseling that is the critical component. You need to understand this and help the client understand this. In other words, **sell the sizzle, not the steak!***

This is a good example of why people who use online resources to create their own documents, prepare documents that are inadequate to meet their goals. Many websites allow individuals to create their own powers of attorney, medical directives, wills, or trusts. The important part of estate planning is not the document that is created from the forms provided. Rather, it is the wisdom of one who is experienced enough to understand and counsel clients concerning their goals and objectives within the bounds of the law. Even more than that, it is having the experience and knowledge to listen to the client. Listen for those facts that bear upon a successful estate plan, but that are not immediately apparent. Asking a series of questions in checklist fashion is destined to meet your agenda of completing a series of documents for the client, but does it address those issues that the client is most concerned about that you never asked about?

Using a checklist to ask a series of leading questions is not the answer for a well-drafted series of documents that really meet the client's objectives. "If, then" logic works when you are dealing with the mechanics of a car, or an engineering project. It can appear to work fine to produce a Will that appears to be legally valid in all fifty states, but does it address the nuances of an individual's personality? Does it delve into the dynamics of the family? Does it factor in all the other areas of law that potentially impact the decisions one makes? Can it address a constantly changing legal environment that changes on a daily basis? Lawyers do this all the time without the client fully appreciating the implications and underpinning of that lawyer's planning. But, this is why engaging an attorney can be so critical to success in the ultimate outcome. The value of that experience cannot be overestimated.

The difference between counseling a client on pet trusts based on my personal experience is somewhat unique to me as a result of my understanding of the law and my personal experience working in a veterinary clinic. My sizzle is my personal experience combined with my knowledge of the law. Your sizzle will be unique to you. Follow along as I help you understand what your sizzle might be.

Focus your practice on those aspects of your experience and training that provide value for the client. What is there about you that will distinguish you from every other practitioner and the resources available online? Remember, family law practice specializing in same sex divorces? Read on.

Chapter 30

Sell the Sizzle, Not the Steak: Part II

Are you a "one off" attorney? This is an attorney who engages a client for the service sought and fails to understand they might be a greater source of business if they were to conduct business in a different manner.

A True Story

Years ago as a sales rep, many of my dealers never got it. I was employed by a company that produced compact diesel tractors. The least successful dealers were the ones who felt they were selling a product—compact diesel tractors. The most successful dealers understood they were really selling a service: long-term business relationships.

The product-focused dealers concentrated on making a certain percentage profit on each tractor. Or it didn't go out the door. Their accountants told them that they had to make 23 percent profit to cover their overhead to stay in business, for instance. They focused almost entirely on price to make the 23 percent profit, and indeed, they were able to sell some units and maintain their margins just as their accountant advised.

The service-focused dealers concentrated on the customer and the customer's needs. Each customer was evaluated based on his or her unique situation. Pricing came up only during the final negotiations. Even if the customer insisted on getting a price quote, the dealer would persist in discussing the features that would satisfy the customer's needs and profile to help the customer understand "value" versus "price." And, these dealers often sold their tractors for even less than the product-focused dealers. But the value-focused dealers understood that with every tractor in the field he sold, he would sell implements to go on that tractor. He would discount the tractor and sell the implements at full price. He would sell even more services later, which benefited the customer and the dealer. In the end, they both benefited.

The service dealer reduced the price up front with an understanding that he would make more in the long run on implements and follow-up service. In doing so, he actually gave the customers greater value by maintaining a working relationship with them. By discounting, he would capture more sales and increase his volume substantially over the product dealers who were shortsighted and only interested in short-term results. As a result, he would get volume discounts on his tractors from the manufacturer above and beyond the normal discounts to the dealers. In addition, a larger volume of customers meant they were more numerous than the product dealers customers. They were likely to tell others that the dealer gave them a really good price on the tractor and more customers would be drawn to the "good deal" dealer.

In my estate planning practice, many of the individuals we meet have trusts or wills that are five years old, ten years old, or even older. They are not returning to the attorney who drafted them as they never established a relationship. Instead, many of those attorneys were focused on "selling the tractor" and forgot about the service aspect of their practice.

You can charge $2,500 or more for a living trust and send the client out the door with a perfectly competent document that meets the client's needs for the moment. However, even if you offered the trust for $1,500 and earned less on that "product," you can still make as much as the attorneys who charge more up front over the life of the relationship. All too often, I see clients who have been serviced and dropped after the fee was collected from the "one off" attorneys. The attorney never bothered to update their client's documents and keep them current. If you charged $1,500 up front and for ten years charged $100 a year for an annual review, the client would get much better service for the money spent. The only difference for you is that you have to wait longer for the income. However, once you establish an ongoing relationship with your clients, your revenue stream will be more predictable and measured over time. In the long run, you would actually make more as a client who was fifty at the time you first counseled him could easily live to be eighty years old. Thirty years at $100 plus the initial income from the documents is greater than you would make by charging $2,500 up front and forgetting about the client.

When a client needed more than a regular checkup for the $100 fee, you would be justified in charging them to modify their estate planning documents to reflect changes in the law. They would be less reluctant to come back to you fearing another $2,500 bill. Even more important, you keep them current with the law and their changed circumstances, which is a huge benefit for them. Compare that to the clients I see cross my doorstep with outdated and ineffective estate plans that often have devastating consequences for those clients.

Think about your approach to client relations and I believe you will prosper and your services will have greater value for your clients as well.

Chapter 31

Is a Niche Practice in Your Future?

As you research your options for practice, how broad should you cast your net?

For fifteen years, I have reached out to law students and practitioners in an attempt to help them succeed in the business of law and reduce avoidable stress in the process. There are many opportunities in this profession to make a good living with proper organization and planning.

The upside of being a general practitioner means that anyone can be a client. Any promotion that you do to sell your services as a "lawyer" will be perceived as fungible. That is, they will be viewed as similar as every other lawyer offering legal advice. If you wish to compete, the only way you can distinguish yourself is by competing on price. Immediately below in bold print, I have copied a list of practice areas that one solo lawyer listed on that solo lawyer's website:

- Family law
- Divorce
- Child custody and support
- Living trust and wills
- Estate planning
- Property law
- Personal injury
- Guardianship
- Civil litigation and more

If you needed someone to represent you in an action for divorce, a divorce where you knew it would be contested and involve custody and complex property division issues, would you consider retaining this attorney? The website simply lists those areas of practice and on a given day, as a client, I would assume that attorney is very busy and distracted with so many areas of practice. Personally, I would look for someone who specialized in divorces. In fact, even if the divorce isn't complex and messy, if I could choose, I would select someone who has greater experience in the subject matter of my greatest concern.

If, however, the attorney represented only clients in divorces and only men, I might be inclined to believe that they have more experience representing male clients in divorce actions. As a result, if they were to tell me that they had a great deal of experience in the issues associated with those types of divorces, I might be inclined to believe them more than if the lawyer from the website where this list was posted were to assert that claim.

If the lawyers who specialize in divorces for male clients charge more for their services, I might be inclined to believe that they are worth it if they tell me they have greater experience in that area of practice. Conversely, a general practitioner can tell me that he or she has a great deal of experience in those matters, but it will likely be a hard sell. So if you want to distinguish yourself in the community where you practice, narrow your field of practice and specialize so that you are not having to compete on price to beat out the competition. Of course, it is always possible to make a name for yourself in a high-profile case and draw attention to your skills in one of many areas of practice so that you can command higher prices for your services. But that is much harder to accomplish.

Unless you narrow your focus and specialize, you will also be using a shotgun approach to reach your audience through your advertising. It will not be a targeted audience. If you narrowly define your area of practice, you can also narrowly define the audience you need to reach and use more targeted advertising to reach them with fewer media sources for less money.

Another disadvantage of being a generalist is that you will need to stay current in multiple fields of law—this is a recipe for potential malpractice.

What is your passion? What do you really love to do? Make that your area of specialization.

Many of the examples in this text are based on estate planning as that is where my experience is greatest. They say "write about what you know," well, I know about estate planning best, so there you go!

What do I mean by a "niche practice"? Why do you hear many advocate this approach and is it right for you? Why is this approach popular?

First, let's consider the day in the life of a "general practitioner." You will find many attorneys who advertise a whole list of areas of practice for which they may be retained. On any given day, they may be involved with a client charged with driving while intoxicated, a client who is seeking a divorce, and a client who wishes to file for bankruptcy. That means those attorneys must keep up to date and current on those three very different areas of law before they render an opinion on how to proceed in each of those cases. And to be fair, those who have been in practice for some time can probably handle each of those different areas of practice competently. But where does it end? For instance, the client seeking a divorce discloses that she is not a U.S. citizen and that she owns significant property outside of the United States. For you to continue to represent that client, either you will have to go beyond your area of comfort and do extensive research, or you will have to refer the matter to someone else or share fees with the client's consent to obtain the necessary expertise since you are not an immigration law attorney.

You also have three different cases with three different courts involved, with different judges, and different groups of attorneys who have expertise in those three areas. You also have three different types of clients who may be attracted as clients through three different methods in the media. It may be that you can handle it and that you have done enough of those types of cases in the past that you feel these are worth taking on since you are trying to maximize your revenue. How far do you go with this? Can you practice in four, five, six, or more areas of law and continue to be competent in them all? Will you be able to keep abreast of the changes in all those areas of law to be a zealous advocate for all of them? Do you risk making mistakes that will ultimately be the basis for a grievance or malpractice claim?

I have interviewed attorneys who say that they practice in a rural area. As a result, they have to be everything to everyone to survive. This is a strategy that they have employed successfully for years and one that they will continue to employ. This would seem to make sense, particularly in a highly competitive legal services environment. The upside to this approach is that you can service virtually anyone who walks in the door. And if they have questions you cannot answer, you can charge them more because it will take longer to find the answer, and you can bill by the hour anyway. Also, the local population will feel comfortable seeking your assistance as you are not likely to turn them away and waste their time or yours. This is the strategy that many attorneys employ and one that you may wish to pursue. However, I would counsel against this approach unless you find that there is no other choice.

The reason this approach is not the best approach, in my opinion, is that the practice of law is potentially so diverse and today, with the Internet, it is possible to cultivate a following and significant business expansion beyond your geographic area even if you limit your areas of practice.

Equine Law: Just One Example of How It Was Done

Long before it was popular to find a niche in legal practice, I encouraged my students to consider defining their practice narrowly. When I first started counseling students, I told them to narrow their focus to two or three substantive areas at most. More recently, I have encouraged them to further define their focus even more. For many reasons, it is far better to define your practice within narrowly defined limits as much as possible because of *efficiency* in practice. One attorney who did just that is Julie Fershtman.

Julie is the past president of the State Bar of Michigan and a very accomplished attorney. She didn't get to where she is by just doing what other lawyers did. Julie graduated from law school with the thought that it might be possible to merge her love and interest in horses with her professional aspirations.

First, she immersed herself in any part of the Michigan Code concerning horse ownership, liability, commerce, or anything else related to horses that she could find. She investigated court cases and developments in the code that had the potential to affect anyone owning, leasing, transporting, or riding horses, or using the equipment associated with horses. Before doing this, Julie was aware that Michigan has a very large population of horses. She understood the kind of issues that horse owners dealt with and decided to become one of the few lawyers in the United States to establish expertise in equine law.

But this meant that she had to take some risk and she decided to ask Jay Foonberg if that area of law might have traction. The reason she asked Mr. Foonberg for his opinion was because he wrote, *How to Start & Build a Law Practice*, which is currently in its sixth edition. In my own experience, that book is often described by practitioners whom I have interviewed as the bible for practice principles. Jay is a heavyweight in the solo practice arena; so Julie sought his advice about an equine law practice.

In Julie's own words:

I asked Jay Foonberg in 1993 whether an Equine Law practice was viable. He replied "no" and told me "I'd starve." That was a challenge; I did it anyway. (NOTE: I also practice commercial litigation, insurance law, insurance defense—not just equine, but much of my business came from my Equine Law work.)

Julie didn't tackle this without a plan. She had dependents and responsibilities. So she set about implementing this plan with persistence, and she had an ability to see the potential for a practice with this specialty.

Diamonds are nothing more than chunks of coal that stuck to their jobs.

Malcolm Forbes

Michigan has a few publications for the horse industry. *Saddle Up! Magazine* is one of them and it is distributed all over Michigan every month. Julie offered to write a column on horses and the law for the magazine each month. She has been doing this since 1993, and though equine law is not her exclusive domain, it has been a productive and unique practice area with very little competition from the start. Even as others have entered the market (I now see others advertising equine law as an area of practice), Julie is the first and foremost expert in equine law. She even travels to other states to make presentations and has been hired as pro hac vice counsel for those affected by developments in this area of the law. She has been able to follow her passion and opened doors for others to follow her example in developing new and creative ways to use a law degree.

Julie has her own blog, www.equinelawblog.com, which you may wish to visit to find out more about this topic or to contact her.

The equine law specialization that Julie Fershtman established is just one example of defining your practice within narrow limits to meet the needs of a discrete population of potential clients. It is possible to distinguish yourself from every other attorney advertising on the Internet. What Julie did was to help people know that they had problems or opportunities that *they didn't know they had* and, most important, *she was the solution*. Once you define yourself in that manner, you are no longer competing with other lawyers on price. If you are the only one offering expertise in their area of concern, pricing goes to the bottom of the list if they need your unique skills and services.

Along with the benefits of greater flexibility in your pricing structure come even greater benefits. Even if you price your services on a par with everyone else, you will experience much greater efficiencies in your business model. For instance, rather than having to advertise to the entire population of a region through newsprint, billboards, radio, or the Internet, you can focus like a laser on a narrow segment of the population. You can target your advertising with a message that is tailored to the specific needs of the individuals who you are trying to reach. The message is much more powerful if it addresses a specific need that your potential client feels must be met.

For example, you might define your practice as an estate planning practice that specializes on the requirements of individuals who have pets and wish to provide for the long-term care of those pets after the client passes away. Go to any supermarket and walk the aisles to see how much space is devoted to nutritional items for babies. Now, go to the area devoted to the nutritional needs of dogs and cats. Which of those sections has more area devoted to it? Where do people place importance? Where do they spend their money? See my point?

Many of the clients I see who are in their sixties and older find that their children have moved out of the area, their friends begin to die off, many spouses are no longer alive or they are divorced. When they come home, do they come home to an empty house? Some do, but many do not. As I describe this situation, think how often you have seen this, maybe not the exact scenario, but something similar.

Grandma comes home to an overweight barking Chihuahua! That dog will bite anyone who walks in the door. It is barking and its tail is wagging for joy that granny has arrived. Not only has she arrived; she has **treats**. *And, she cooks his food and mashes it because the dog has lost half of his teeth. When you meet with her to talk about her estate planning options and ask her about the disposition of her assets, she will be engaged and give you directions to divide her property in various ways. If you ask her if she has any pets, she will light up and, not only tell you that she has a dog, she will give you his name and tell you stories about how much she loves that dog and how it will not leave her side when she comes home.*

You may want to consider specializing within a specialty. How would this work? You are an estate planning attorney, but with a twist. You prepare estate plans with particular emphasis on the care and comfort of clients' pets after the owners are gone. You focus on the laws relating to the transfer of assets after death to trusts for the care of animals. In Michigan, we have laws allowing for the creation of trusts that effectively leave property to things (animals) called "pet trusts." Focusing on this narrow area of specialization gives you the ability to market your services to individuals with special needs. How would you reach them? Meet with the local veterinarians and offer to do seminars for their clients explaining various arrangements that can be made through estate plans for their pets.

Educate them on some of the concerns they might have as those plans are implemented and how you can make sure that their concerns are addressed. Get detailed information in your files concerning the name of the treating veterinarian. Get a release from your client to allow their agent to access their pet's records after the client passes away. What are their pets' favorite foods, allergies, toys, and habits? You could also go to commercial pet supply retailers, local animal shelters, senior centers, and offer to do presentations to discuss these considerations for planning purposes.

By setting yourself apart from everyone else and defining your market narrowly, you will limit your competition. You can alert potential clients to the fact that they had a problem they didn't know they had and you are the solution. Price becomes secondary as you are offering a valuable and unique service that is important to them.

As an estate planning attorney, you might specialize in the transition of farms in the family, cottage trusts, gun trusts, estate planning for same sex couples, estate planning for couples without children, or for couples with in-vitro produced children, and so forth. What is it that you are passionate about? Write about it and publish articles explaining to the public special considerations when counseling them about their estate plans.

What I just described is a way that you can define your practice subject matter narrowly. By the same token, you can define yourself within segments of the population based on their particular needs. For instance, you could offer your services for homebound clients. You could set up your office to accommodate individuals with visual, hearing, or other physical impairments. You might want to focus on certain ethnic populations or families with loved ones in prison. Everywhere you look, there are individuals with special needs that need to be addressed. Or you could specialize in representing individuals affected by new developments in the law or technology. For instance, new developments in technology are not only providing greater access and flexibility for practitioners, they are also creating new opportunities for specialization. In the spring of 2016, I attended the ABA TechShow, as I have for the past five years. The watchword at the convention was "security" and how we need to protect our clients from unwanted intrusions and disclosures of their private information. Today there are developments and opportunities for risk managers, security auditors, and specialists in electronic discovery. Robotics, unmanned vehicles, drones, and access to digital files after death by family members all present new challenges and opportunities to develop practices or consultants who specialize in those areas, just to name a few. For the populations who might be concerned or interested in those developing areas of law or management, you need to think:

- Where do they gather? Be there.
- What do they read? Write articles for those periodicals.
- What are their special needs? Define them and offer solutions.

Wherever and however you appear, give your potential audience something they will value—your appreciation and understanding of their special needs. And you have to inform them that you have the solutions. You don't need to hard sell your services. Just make them aware that you are sensitive to their needs and you can solve their problems and they will come seeking your advice when they perceive the need. This approach takes some patience as once the seeds are planted, not all of them will take root immediately. But good business takes a plan, patience, execution, and follow-through to succeed.

If you use this approach, you will have defined and branded your services. You will distinguish yourself from all the "also rans." Look at what other attorneys are doing, and do it differently.

Establish a practice model that is competitive where you practice law. One that is sustainable over the long term, and is grounded in sound legal and financial principles. Much of the work establishing your expertise can be accomplished while you're still a student; in fact, it's important that you engage in that preparatory work now, before you graduate. Very few students who I meet have given thought to ways that they may establish themselves before graduation. You can establish a presence with the group of individuals where your expertise will be valued and that can set the stage for your financial success later on.

Start with a plan that gives you an edge over your competitors and removes you from the strategy of discounted legal services. Specialize in an area of law that interests you and you will find that you will look forward to the challenges that are presented. You will realize greater efficiency and become the authority in the area for clients who come to you for your expertise, not your reduced fees. This is what I mean by "selling the sizzle." Rather than selling a Will like everyone else, you offer skills to produce an estate plan tailored to a unique need and pricing becomes secondary.

Chapter 32

Carnegie Skills

Do You Have Them? How Important Are They in Your Practice?

Dale Carnegie authored a book *How to Win Friends and Influence People,* which is designed to help the reader improve the ability to deal with others effectively. Frankly, if you have not read it, it is one book you might want to consider for your review. It was first published in 1936 and continues to be popular today.

The reason it continues to be popular is that the advice between the covers is just as sound today as it was when it was first put in print. Millions of copies have been sold because anyone reading it will soon be struck with the simplicity of the message; but it is a message that many students and attorneys fail to understand. The book gives simple rules to live by and they are obvious to one reading the book. However, we are all guilty of forgetting to implement the principles identified.

The Carnegie book includes advice, such as:

- *Show respect for the other person's opinions. Never say "You're wrong."*
- *Arouse in the other person an eager want.*
- *Remember that a person's name is, to that person, the sweetest and most important sound in any language.*
- *Be a good listener. Encourage others to talk about themselves.*
- *The only way to get the best of an argument is to avoid it.*

As you read these and all the principles in the book you will be struck again about the simplicity of the message. But it is all about putting the focus on others, and away from yourself. They really boil down to respect for others, regardless of your differences and allowing others to express their feelings and listening to them without interruption and with an open mind.

With the Internet and social media, the one thing that is missing that Carnegie's book emphasizes is personal interaction on a level that is absent through the Internet. To those students who have excellent social skills, I tell them that they have the Carnegie skills and I can often predict their success based upon their ability to engage others with those skills. It is not their skill as a lawyer and their intellect that wins over clients. It is the ability to connect with their clients and that is what that book is all about.

Read the book; it will help you to understand the most important principles to help you find success in your practice. Dale Carnegie Training offers extensive coaching using the principles presented in the book. See http://www.dalecarnegie.com/events/dale_carnegie_course/.

Chapter 33

Uber into Law: Access Docs from Anywhere

Uber into Law? A True Story

In April of 2016, and again during August, I found myself in Chicago in need of transportation. I downloaded the Uber app and quickly found myself using Uber to move about the city seamlessly.

In the event you have not used Uber, unlike conventional taxis that you can flag down at the curb, you have to use your smartphone with the Uber app to identify where you are located when you need a ride. Then you wait for an Uber driver to signal a fare.

That driver's vehicle shows up on your smartphone screen within the city grid, moving across the streets as it approaches you. You see a small timer with the number of minutes estimated for arrival, and also a very small picture of the driver, the vehicle license number, and the make of the vehicle that will be picking you up.

For each of my rides (about fifteen in total), I took the opportunity to ask drivers about their experience and how much they were making, on average. I will not quote figures, but they were pretty impressive. And all of the drivers expressed satisfaction with Uber and the Uber program. Mothers, with children in school, could drop the kids off and drive throughout the day. Then they could check out and pick up their kids from school. One driver was saving money for her wedding by driving before and after she reported for her full-time job. A number of former cabbies who I rode with were driving for Uber because of the money and flexibility of that program.

The ability to check in and out as you please and to operate as an independent contractor (unless defined otherwise in the courts) was a great draw. In addition, no money changes hands with Uber, as your ride is charged to a credit card account that Uber keeps on file. They discourage tipping, so drivers generally do not carry cash. Their vehicles were all very clean and are checked out by Uber before they sign on a driver. I was told that cars could not be over ten years old and had to go through a safety check. The payment for the driver is made each week into the driver's account and Uber keeps 20 percent.

As I attended the ABA Annual Meeting in Chicago, it occurred to me that a recent grad who is waiting for Bar results, or someone starting out with extra time on their hands, could Uber for income until they got their practice up and running.

Think about it. If you were paperless (it has so many advantages) and your software was in the cloud, you would be able to access your files from anywhere. Further, with a laptop and smartphone, if a client called, you could either have an answering service or use Google Voice to transcribe any voicemails. After your fare (if you are occupied), you could immediately check out of Uber, park, and conduct your business from your car. You can use a number of available call forwarding apps so that your client will not know where you are, or what phone you call from when you respond to an incoming call. Besides, clients are accustomed to speaking with their attorneys who are constantly on the go.

This gives you the opportunity to obtain a constant stream of income while you develop your business. You could Uber early in the day and late in the evening. You could Uber on weekends. From the conversations I had with drivers, those times were the most productive times for income in any event. Uber offers to link you with local auto dealers and will help you with the financing of a vehicle. But, you might even be able to drive your current vehicle. One of my drivers was driving a car with 130,000 miles on the odometer. He said he had to have it inspected, and several maintenance items were necessary, before he could put it into service. But he said, after the inspection and work he had done on it, it never ran better.

So if you have a clean driving record and are able to operate from a mobile office, you might be a candidate to Uber into solo practice. Check it out. It might be an option to help finance your startup. There is no shame in working a job on the side to get yourself established. And this type of work has the advantage of being very flexible. With the technology available today, you have so much more flexibility than lawyers had even ten years ago.

Chapter 34

Wholesale Versus Retail: Keep Your Eye on the Ball and Expand Your Reach and Influence

Are you operating at maximum efficiency? What is your target audience and how do you reach them?

Measure your marketing efficiency by the amount of time you spend reaching your target audience and the amount of sales you close on account of your efforts. Are you focusing on retail and missing wholesale opportunities?

An example of retail marketing is what many long-term practitioners frequently refer to as "word of mouth" referrals. These are former clients who refer business to those attorneys without further effort by the lawyer. Senior practitioners will often refer to that method of marketing as their primary source of business. This is understandable as they opened their practices at a time when yellow pages and newspaper ads were the most commonly employed methods of reaching potential clients.

As they became more established, existing clients would refer others to those attorneys who proved to be effective and to provide great service. But the yellow pages and newsprint are no longer the most effective ways to reach newer generations of potential clients. Those outclassed modes of advertising wane in comparison to more efficient digital methods of marketing today. And many older attorneys, unwilling to adapt to the digital age, continue to rely upon "word of mouth" advertising. Indeed, they continue to get referrals—but at an ever decreasing rate.

Retail marketing is also manifested in direct contact with potential clients through one-on-one contact through membership in church groups, fraternal organizations, or other social interaction. However, your time to do that can be limited. So, how do you expand your sphere of influence with greater efficiency?

Some of this is intuitively obvious—use the Internet and blog, and connect with LinkedIn, Tweet, Facebook, and so on. There are other ways to reach multiple potential clients. And if you can link your contact to a personal endorsement you will most likely beat the competition. There is another form of wholesale sales that can be even more powerful than Internet referrals.

FindLaw 2014 Consumer Legal Needs Survey Marketing PowerPoint[1] demonstrates the power of personal referrals. What are the most important influencing factors? Price was only a fraction of the equation influencing buying decisions, whereas expertise, personal recommendations, and creating a sense of trust outweighed cost by a wide margin, if all three were combined. All three of those factors can be enhanced by a referral from another professional such as a Certified Public Accountant who recommends you to his or her established client.

You will see that even though the focus of this survey is on the use of Internet resources for searches, *personal relationship building* is the essence of long-term growth and results in the greatest success in closing the deal ultimately. Instead of going to the end users, one by one, seeking their business, go to a business that deals with the same clientele that you engage and establish relationships with them. Encourage them to refer clients to your office from their client base.

For example, if you are an estate planning attorney, CPAs, insurance agents, social workers, financial planners, and even funeral home representatives serve many of the same people who you seek to represent. Do you spend time cultivating relationships with those individuals in your community? This has potentially greater reach and a multiplying effect as compared to end user contacts. There may be a significant lag time between your outreach and a referral, but don't be dismayed as it is "all numbers." The more quality relationships you establish, the greater your likelihood of success later on.

Now carry the efficiency of one CPA as a referral source working for you and selling your services beyond that, one more level. Have you considered doing presentations to gatherings of those individuals? The recent Supreme Court ruling on same sex marriages, for instance, is an example of an opportunity to reach out and provide guidance on how that decision may affect them and their clients. What are you waiting for? Provide information that will help them appear better informed among their client base. Put together a

---

1. PowerPoint is availale at http://www.slideshare.net/FindLawLawyerMarketing/findlaw-2014-us-consumer-legal-needs-survey-37061283.

fact sheet concerning IRS rulings and how this recent decision may affect possible outcomes as the recent Supreme Court decision works its way through the courts. Give something of value to them, and they will repay the favor.

As a result, they may refer clients to you for the effort you expended on their behalf. A crowd of CPAs has the potential to send you numerous clients whereas a meeting with a single CPA might yield clients, but not in the numbers you can cultivate through a presentation before a group of CPAs. Meeting with a single CPA is wholesale, but not on the scale that a crowd would yield. That is even more efficient use of your time and once you prepare a fact sheet for one CPA, it can be distributed to multiple CPAs with little additional effort.

So consider the multiplier effect of one-on-one client contact, which is enhanced by one-on-one professional referral source, which is enhanced by one-on-several referral sources, and spend your time expanding your sphere of influence.

Chapter 35

Would You Buy a Car Without Wheels? Understand What You Are Selling: It Isn't Paper

Think about it, would you purchase a car from someone who would have nothing to do with it after you left the lot? They would sell you the car and say, "we can't help you after you leave the lot regarding the maintenance or service of the car. And we won't carry any parts either." Of course, they would have to sell it greatly discounted and even then you would be wondering how long you could drive it before you needed the essential services to keep it running later.

But look at certain websites and consider this—you see forms for the preparation and production of wills, trusts, business formation, and so forth. What is missing at those websites is the paperwork for the execution of those documents. Of course, they offer to connect you with lawyers of their choosing (and extract addition money from that lawyer for the privilege, who then passes those costs on to you paying extra fees to the Internet platform provider which you get to subsidize).

A True Story

The other day I was reading a thread on one of the listservs that I monitor concerning a bank teller informing an attorney that a person cannot be a successor trustee on a trust until the settlor has passed away. As a result, the teller would not accept documentation that enabled the successor to manage that account without an intervention by the successor's attorney who spoke with the bank's legal counsel to correct the teller's misunderstanding.

Here is where the wheels come off: the individual who would go online and draft a document transferring authority to their agent as successor is left without knowing if the teller was right or wrong. It is in the EXECUTION of the document or fostering the goals of the individual that results in "self-helpers" running into trouble later on. They find that they need an attorney to unravel the mess that many of them created in the first instance. And the "cost savings" they realized at first are spent many times over cleaning up the mess they created.

You will find plenty of websites that walk you through the preparation of a will, but try to find documents on that same website that give you the forms to probate that will and you will find yourself stranded. The reason is that those providers know that each jurisdiction is going to be different. They understand that there is no single solution or format for the unexpected and undefined circumstances that are likely to confront a person in probate. You need someone with knowledge and experience who can fashion documents that meet the demands of uncertainty that dominate the legal system.

So the next time a client says, "I can do my own will on the Internet for a lot less," say, "That is fine, but when you decide you want the 'wheels,' come back and see me. I sell the whole unit."

Chapter 36

Cost-Effective Mediocrity: Make Sure You Invest Your Money Wisely in Marketing Your Firm

Penny Wise?

Running your business, be careful that the cost savings you experience may move you rapidly to cost-efficient mediocrity. Within the context of many organizations, decisions from the top can move an organization toward a more "efficient" business model that is "mean and lean." Yet they undermine the fundamental service aspect of the business so that cost savings turns out to be easy cuts that paralyze the vital organs of the business and contribute to its demise.

This pattern has been repeated many times in business models that are driven by cost accounting without the vision necessary to see the impact on the consumer and slow progression to the organization's demise. Unfortunately, by the time it is clear that the cuts that were critical to satisfy the bean counters' mandates, they have taken the company into a death spiral, which is discovered too late.

A True Story Bears Repeating

Years ago, when I was in sales, I had dealers who were instructed by their accountants to hold the product (tractors) until they made 23 percent margin on each piece of equipment. The accountants explained to those dealers that it was essential to cover their overhead. I could visit those dealers and find they would sit on inventory for six months or more and pay interest to cover the floor plan costs. In the end, if they sold it, they may have held their price, but their margin continued to shrink as they held out for their price and paid floor plan interest.

Other dealers took the stand that if they got a piece of equipment and could turn it around and make 5 percent within a week or two, they sold it. It was much less than 23 percent, but it was almost pure profit. Even though the customer sought the discount on the tractor, they often would be willing to pay full price on the attachments.

Now, I am not suggesting you discount your services. In fact, I would argue the opposite. But to succeed, you will need to help your clients understand the value of your services and be willing to do value billing (set fees for particular services) as opposed to hourly billing. If you don't know it, value billing is an increasing trend and one that the clients appreciate because of predictability. Look not at the initial pricing; rather look beyond that to the total package that the client may purchase in the end if you put them on a maintenance program for a full review of their estate planning documents, for instance, every two years. Changes in the law and family associations mean that estate planning documents should not be static. Being someone's lawyer for life will cause people to say that "I have an attorney." This promotes your firm and the future business that that satisfied client may refer to your office. Some of the best sources of business are your existing clients and referrals that they can bring in. And value billing coupled with efficiency using technology can actually bring in more income than hourly billing.

How many tasks can you accomplish using document assembly in an hour versus what is the maximum hourly rate you can reasonably charge for your services? If you charge $2,000 for a trust and with document assembly software, you might be able to prepare a trust in 30 minutes. If you could do two per hour, that is $4,000 an hour. Can you charge those rates for most routine legal work? I am not suggesting that you will bill $4,000 an hour for 2,000 hours a year. If you could, that would be $8 million. But if you could bill $300 an hour for 2,000 hours, that would max out at $600,000. Think about it—value billing will win out almost every time.

Chapter 37

Do-It-Yourself Lawyering and How It Might Go Awry

A True Story

There is always an easy solution to every human problem—neat, plausible, and wrong.

H. L. Mencken

While waiting for my case to be called in court a few years ago, the judge called the next case. An attorney, with his client at counsel table, informed the judge that they were seeking formal admission of a decedent's will, but there was a problem.

"What problem?" the judge asked.

"Words were crossed out in the will."

"What words?" the judge inquired.

"Of sound mind"

And with that, there was an audible groan throughout the courtroom.

"But, I can explain," said the attorney.

"Please do," said the judge looking flummoxed.

"My client, who is seated next to me, was present when his father went to a credit union to have his will notarized. The teller said that since the witnesses signed below a statement that the testator was an 'adult, and of sound mind,' that she couldn't authenticate that document. She was not able to determine if the testator was of 'sound mind' or not since she wasn't a psychologist. She would only agree to notarize the document if she could cross out the words, 'of sound mind' and that is why those words are struck out, your honor."

The judge could see that this was a case of a lay person trying to give legal advice. The judge understood that the oath taken by the notary was acknowledgment by the witnesses as to what they believed and the veracity of their statements had no bearing on what the notary believed. She was only authenticating that the person signing was who they said they were and that they were swearing to certain facts in her presence.

When someone takes an oath in court to tell the truth, the person may or may not tell the truth. But the function of the bailiff is essentially the same as the notary. He or she documents the fact, in open court, that both the plaintiff and the defendant swear to tell the truth under penalty of perjury.

On this occasion the judge looked about the courtroom and said, "Anyone here appearing to object to a motion for the admission of this will?" There was silence. Then, he went on to say, "Hearing no objection, so ordered." So there is a will on record that purports to deny that the testator is competent. That will was used as the basis for distribution of the decedent's property under the laws of the State of Michigan.

As I often tell my students, "That may not be the law, but unless you appeal the order of a judge, it is the law to you."

Why do lawyers exist? To help clients understand that the law is not intuitive and not for the faint of heart. Often when we see examples of nonlawyers explaining the law to others, we just shake our heads. The teller who notarized that will was probably never made aware of the problems she caused, and it took an attorney to unravel the mess. The client in this instance understood the consequence of "do-it-yourself lawyering," but how many of your clients really understand the value of your education, experience, and wise counsel? It is up to you to help them see their way to value your services. Share this story with them as just one example of self-help lawyering to reinforce for them the value of your services.

Chapter 38

Dog in a Basket: One More Way to Think About How to Sell Your Service and Close the Sale

"Can't Do That on LegalZoom™"

The title in quotes above appears on a T-shirt that my students gave me, which has the LegalZoom™ logo on it. Above the logo, they penned in felt tip marker, "Can't do that on." They also signed it on the back. The reason they gave me that shirt is that they heard me describe how online legal services are not always the best possible alternative for individuals during my estate planning class.

Don't get me wrong, many individuals would not seek the services of a lawyer due to the cost and, without LegalZoom™, they would not seek assistance of any sort. Some individuals will always look for more efficient ways to accomplish their goals. And, to their credit, LegalZoom™ is one of the entities providing a service that appears to have met an unmet need. Many lawyers see this and other legal access sites as their impending doom and a major game changer for legal services for the future. I see it somewhat differently.

A True Story Repeated for Emphasis

As a high school student fifty years ago, I was employed at a veterinary clinic on weekends. At that clinic, there were over sixty cages that were used to house animals who were recovering from medical interventions. The majority of them, however, were used to board animals for a fee. One of my tasks was to take the animals (usually dogs) and put them in "runs" so they could get exercise.

Meanwhile, I cleaned their cages and refreshed their water and food. One of the animals boarded almost every weekend was a German Shepherd. The "owners" would bring the dog to the clinic for the weekend and pick him up on Mondays.

Let me describe that animal. He was a full-grown German Shepherd and always carried into the clinic in a padded basket. The reason he didn't come in on a leash was that he couldn't walk. In fact, all he did was lie on his side. Periodically, using the muscles of the trunk of his body, he would rise a few inches. He was paralyzed in his extremities. His eyes would often be matted and it was essential that he be placed on a lamb's fleece and turned periodically. I was astonished at the condition of this dog when I first saw him and asked the veterinarian why this was so?

The vet explained that that couple had been charged with the care of this dog after the owner had passed away. He said that it was his understanding that they were being paid a monthly stipend to care for the dog as long as it lived. He also explained that the affliction of that animal occurred after the original owner had passed away.

Personally, I found it objectionable that they would keep that dog alive. As I look back, and as a skeptic, I feel their motives were questionable. I feel that the money was the object of their affection, not the welfare of that dog.

There is a lesson here. Unintended consequences may flow from your carefully laid plans, as in this case. Be careful what you wish for! You love your pet and put in place what you believe are safeguards to protect your dog after you pass away. You establish a pet trust to ensure that your dog is cared for after you are gone. As a result of this experience, if I established a trust for a pet, I would provide for a trusted, uncompensated, third party with powers to intervene and terminate the trust under certain circumstances consistent with the welfare of the animal.

But that advice is personal to me and would flow from my legal education and experience. The owner of that dog would have probably been horrified at the outcome and no cost would be too great to prevent such a miscarriage of their intent.

"Can't Get That on LegalZoom™"

This brings me to the text that happens to be on my T-shirt and the connection to this story. I hear many attorneys lament the development of legal resources on the Internet and the potential they have to affect their bottom line. I couldn't disagree more. Examples like the one above demonstrate that there will always be a place for good legal counsel that cannot be accessed online.

All of my students inquire of their clients whether they have any pets to help the client make well-reasoned decisions concerning their care after the client dies. The least valuable outcome for any client is the document itself. It is the counseling that goes into informed decision making and execution on that plan that has the greatest value. It really requires someone experienced enough to see the potential "parade of horrors" that may dominate the ultimate outcomes of a client's best laid plans. If they choose to do it on their own, they risk the "dog in a basket" outcome.

And after the person dies, who will probate the estate? The counseling before preparation and later execution of that plan is where the greatest skill must be employed. As you will notice, even websites of self-prepared documents offer to connect the applicant with attorneys for the legal advice who that person may wish to consult. The problem is that the self-help individual may not have the ability to understand that there are legal or practical considerations that can only be the product of education and experience. They might not understand the importance of consultation with an attorney as they won't recognize the issue in the first place, as in the case of the story above.

Recently one of my students came back from the Register of Deeds Office in our county. When the Registrar heard the student say that she was in her third year of law school, the Registrar told her to try to get individuals to seek her services in drafting their deeds. The reason for this was that the Registrar's office gave blank deeds to individuals who sought them as a service to the community. As long as those deeds were in "record-able form" the Registrar was obligated to record them. However, she explained, "they are usually full of errors in the legal descriptions or types of estates granted." And the Registrar is prohibited from giving legal advice. So she must record those "messes" as she described them. She found it extremely frustrating to see this going on, but could not intercede or offer any legal advice. Those individuals would never think to seek the advice of an attorney, since the deed was recorded. In their minds the act of recording sanctioned their efforts. They didn't realize that they produced a document that would give others all sorts of problems later on.

Many of the errors introduced or poor planning decisions eventually will play out in some fashion. True, some are harmless and can be rectified without too much difficulty. But how many of those errors cost more in the rectification than they would've cost if they were done right in the first place without bypassing an attorney? The solution is better public awareness by the State Bar or the ABA of the types of legal conundrums people routinely find themselves in. Everyday another example of misplaced or misunderstood actions by nonattorneys crosses my desk.

The Lesson for You

If you have been in practice for any length of time, you know the value of good counsel. You know of the problems that you have helped your clients avoid. But the problem is that those very same clients don't fully appreciate the harm they sidestepped by using a lawyer. We need to do a better job of helping the potential client understand why a lawyer's knowledge and experience in the process is "invaluable." Tell them a "true story" of your own so they understand the value of your service. Remember, simply convincing clients that they need a will is no longer enough. You also need to help them understand some of the considerations you have engaged in to be able to complete the final document. You also need to help them understand how, as the preparer, you will be in the best position to execute on those directions later due to the close relationship that you have with your client and insight into their wishes. The counseling that goes into preparing a document with the appropriate agent can make the difference between a seamless transition of property after death or a disaster. Choose the wrong agent and they can literally destroy the principal's intent by fostering bad feelings among those involved. I tell students I can take a poorly drafted document with a great agent and have better results than a well-drafted document with a terrible agent. It is the counseling in helping select appropriate agents for the task at hand that has value, not only the language in the document. You don't get that counseling on Internet sites for the most part.

Chapter 39

Your Tiger Team: One Way to Expand Your Sphere of Influence with Greater Efficiency

Do you want to enhance your effectiveness and impact larger numbers of potential clients?

Here is one idea how to expand your sphere of influence. Establish informal relationships with other attorneys in your area who are not practicing in your area of specialization. Look for attorneys who you would hire based on their reputation and performance. Identify those who deal in a specialty different from your own. See if they are interested in a loose association with you and others to create a "Tiger Team."

The purpose of this group is to enhance the ability of all members of your group to be more competitive and to help one another to build upon the marketing efforts of one another through cross-referrals. This is a fraternity or sorority of sorts. To be part of your group, do your due diligence to determine the quality of work that they are doing. What type of reputation do they have with the judges? With whom do they deal on a regular basis? What about the court clerks? What opinion do they have of the attorneys you are considering for your group? Put the word out that you are developing a group and try to find leaders in the legal community to assist you with recommendations and ideas. Once you have done your background work, then it is time to send out some invitations. Try to meet them one on one at first to see how they feel about a loose association. What organizations do they belong to and do they have any leadership positions with those groups? Have they published any materials? Are those materials referenced or followed? If they are litigators, have they successfully appealed cases before the higher courts in your jurisdiction?

As you develop your group, help them understand that you can all end up with a greater sum than all the parts and that the synergy of a coherent group can lead to greater business for all and greater efficiencies in marketing their practice with more outreach and ability to expand everyone's range of services.

Most important, I try to emphasize developing areas of specialization or niches so that you don't need to gain or maintain expertise in a broad range of subject matter. The downside of that approach is that you will also not be able to serve the client who wants a divorce when you only do estate planning. Or you will have to turn away someone who needs to file for bankruptcy when you only do criminal defense work. So the good news is that your practice will be more efficient. The bad news is that you will limit the number of individuals who will seek your services. But you can offset your self-imposed limitations concerning the subject matter that is the core area of your practice by connecting with others who practice in the areas of law which you have chosen not to enter. But, it also means that your group will be able to do cross-referrals to one another with total confidence that you are sending your client to a competent attorney.

This is not a boutique practice. A boutique practice is one in which you associate with others outside of your area of expertise, typically all within the same law firm with each of the members of the firm conducting legal services for a very narrowly defined population with specialized knowledge in a very well-defined area of the law. I am suggesting you go beyond a law firm model or referral base to vet the attorneys or others who could assist your clients so that your referrals are only made to those individuals who can be relied upon to do excellent legal work for the clients you refer to them. The other component of this system is to have an agreement that everyone will stick to their specialty and not breach that agreement. You do not practice in the same office or hold yourself out as a firm of specialized lawyers. Instead, this is a loose association of attorneys who practice in key, noncompetitive areas of practice. The relationship between the attorneys is based on the consensus that each does what he or she does best. So when you are a family law practitioner and a client needs estate planning, or post-divorce assistance, you would refer that matter out to the expert on your team to do the estate plan for your post-divorce client. The only real way to enforce this arrangement is through voluntary cooperation. This is because there is really no way that you can police others in your group. Nor do you want to have to do that.

Here is a hypothetical scenario: You have decided to do estate planning primarily focused on the transition of businesses to family members. This is more than a niche (estate planning); it narrows the field to estate planning for individuals who have businesses (what I call a micro-niche). Within your group, there will be others who do estate planning for young families with minor children or children with disabilities. One element of this arrangement is that there is a willingness to narrowly define each member's practice areas. For this to work, you cannot go beyond your exclusive venue for practice. Otherwise, if a client came in for estate planning without a clear definition of their goals and objectives, it would be easy to be retained for estate planning and proceed to do a business transition plan when that isn't your specialty.

Members could share resources, but most important is that they need to be willing to share clients. This is not an easy mandate to follow for most practitioners who need to pay their bills.

Too many attorneys, out of concern for a client suing them due to a bad referral, will give more than one name and let the client choose the attorney from several options. Why do that, when you can help your client find a truly competent attorney? And your client will value your opinion if you are clear and firm in making a recommendation.

You may also want to consider expanding the group to include CPAs, financial planners, social workers, and others who might be able to assist your clients. You could meet periodically as a group to find ways to improve your purchasing power, seek discounts through coordinated purchases, and develop strategies to improve everyone's bottom line. It may be possible to join forces to do public service in the name of several underlying sponsors without having to be at every event yourself. Use others with common interests to leverage your business and expand your influence.

Part IV

Miscellaneous Good-to-Know Stuff

Chapter 40

Why Aren't You Going Paperless?

As I send students into the field, they often comment on the law offices that they visit that are "buried in files," files piled on the desk of the attorney. They describe files on the floor, chairs, couches, and file cabinets—everywhere with files piled on top of them for filing.

Before I send them into the field I tell them the story of a presentation by one of the best techno-lawyers I know of, Barron Henley, and his presentation, which I attended, at the ICLE Solo Institute. The presentation was "How to Access Your Documents from Anywhere," or a title very similar to that.

Mr. Henley asked the 200 or so lawyers in the audience how many of them were paperless. About one-half of the hands in the audience were raised when he formed and amplified a puzzled look on his face. He then said, "So why are the rest of you in here?" He went on to explain that if your documents are in hard copy only and not scanned, the only way you or anyone else can access them is to have them physically in your hands. You can't access them simultaneously with anyone else; you cannot access them from out of your office, unless you make copies or bring them with you wherever you wish to access them. If you want to access them, you have to find them first. In paper form, unless you have an extremely well-organized and established method of filing, it might be difficult to find the file and the document within the file quickly. And all of that assumes it is filed in the cabinet and not on a couch in your office or in a pile on the floor.

With the cost of paper, ink, copiers, maintenance costs, and time to file and retrieve constantly on the rise, it just doesn't make sense to maintain paper files anymore. There are excellent programs for retrieval of documents that have been saved electronically. Even if your coding system for your files is not artfully done, those programs can retrieve documents from anywhere very quickly by simply using search terms that are included anywhere in the document. The name of the client as a search term along with the type of the case and any word that relates to the subject matter of the case is enough to retrieve it or a series of documents with those words incorporated.

In order for this to work, first, you need to establish a systematic way of scanning EVERYTHING that comes into your office, and with rare exceptions, shred the originals. Use a scanner that has OCR capability. This means that it can be searched not as bits of storage as 1 or 0, but as discrete and retrievable words that will be recognized when you do a search.

It also means that if you are not the only employee for your office, everyone who works there must "buy in" to the program. If they do not, they will undermine the entire process. You also need to be confident of the technology where this information is saved and it must be backed up so that it can be retrieved later. However, if it is not saved in the cloud, you will not be able to access that information from everywhere. Retrieval from everywhere is a great feature that gives you the ultimate flexibility. You can be in court, on the beach, or sitting on your bed fighting off a cold and still be connected to your office and access your documents without significant down time. Of course, this can be a double-edged sword in that you cannot get away from it at times when you may need some respite. So be careful how you use it; don't abuse it. Remember, you may have a spouse who may not appreciate your "connectedness."

In addition to access by you, your clients can also access their documents through a secure portal or a shared drive. That way you can keep them informed and save the cost of postage and make them feel you are working hard on their behalf.

Finally, the cost savings can be enormous and in the event of a disaster, you can recover very quickly. Hurricane Katrina was a wake-up call for many attorneys who practiced in affected areas. Those who were paper based were put out of business for a very long time, whereas those who were paperless were able to be up and running the next day.

The cost and liability for loss of paper files can be very high. Eliminate the file cabinets and the space necessary to store them and you get the point. Also, have you priced ink cartridges lately? You can purchase ink-jet printers very economically. The reason they are priced so low is that the profit is in the ink. Someone said in the past that the cost of ink is one of the most expensive liquids you can buy, even more expensive than Champagne.

So, if cost, efficiency, accessibility, client satisfaction, or liability for loss in disaster scenarios aren't enough for you, then stay with a paper-based system. But if you are interested in greater efficiency and wish to improve your bottom line, then consider going paperless.

Chapter 41

Not Enough Time for Your Ferrari? Maybe Outsourcing Help Is More Efficient

Never enough time out of the office to drive your Ferrari™? Oh, you don't have a Ferrari? Keep reading my posts and you might be able to afford one if owning one is your goal.

Time is the one commodity that we cannot escape as it wages battle with us on a daily basis. We never have enough time to do everything we want to do. And nobody can be trusted to do the job as well as we do it.

Don't judge each day by the harvest you reap, but by the seeds you sow.

Robert Louis Stevenson

Learn to delegate and you will accomplish so much more. Those tasks that others can do without a license will save you money and allow you to ply your trade for greater returns and leave ministerial tasks to be done by others equipped to do those tasks. Often they can do them better and those you empower will train you how to be more effective at delegation. This is a skill too many of us have failed to exercise or perfect.

Delegate All Sorts of Tasks for $5

Go to https://www.fiverr.com/ and you will see that fiverr® may be an inexpensive solution to allow you to delegate tasks at a cost ($5) that will amaze you for the professional services provided.

For instance, you can have someone create a logo, film a promo, create a jingle, or create a video with a professional model. Of course, $5 is the starting point; but you would be surprised what you can accomplish for that amount of money. Look for other ways to extend your reach.

Those of you who are concerned that nobody will do the task as well as you can do it, get over it. You will never be able to help them perfect their skills if you keep doing everything yourself. What sense does it make for you to do billing that a high school student can do for $10 an hour when you are distracted from completing a task that you are billing at $200 an hour. Often you can find very talented individuals and increase their responsibilities and by doing so, train them and yourself to be more codependent. In the process, you will find that learning to be clear in your instructions and expectations is critical. A person's failure to meet your expectations is often the result of your failure to explain with sufficient clarity what you want accomplished.

The more you practice this art the more you will find you can delegate more than you ever thought possible. Don't forget to compliment and acknowledge superior performance when you experience it. Praise in public and discipline in private is a good rule of thumb.

Consider hiring high school students who have a desire to go to law school some day. Check out fiverr® and keep your eyes open for other opportunities to shift some of your daily doable tasks to others and spend your time billing for tasks that can only be done by a licensed professional and maybe you will find yourself spending more time in your Ferrari!

Chapter 42

Why Your Next Hire Might Come from Starbucks

When you need to hire someone, take them for a test ride before you make an offer.

That Cup of Coffee Might Not Be the Best Thing You Get!

If you are just starting out in practice on your own, it is best to keep your overhead as low as possible. With phone system integration using systems like RingCentral® for $24.99/month, you can maintain control while out of the office to all of your incoming calls without a telephone answering service. At the same time, you can minimize your overhead and avoid having to hire someone to answer phones. When you find you are unable to spend time billing at your professional rates due to administrative distractions that can be done by someone at much less than you can bill, then it might be time to consider part-time or full-time help.

When you reach that point in your business development, how do you find good employees? I once knew a credit union manager who said she hired tellers based on her experiences in retail. She said there are times when you encounter a retail clerk who goes the "extra mile" when they are not being observed by management and, if possible, she would try to observe them more than once. Those were the times when she would get that person's contact information for future reference when she needed to fill a teller slot. As she described it: "I can always train someone to be a teller, but I cannot train someone to have good interpersonal skills or to be motivated." (What I referred to as the Dale Carnegie skills earlier.) That philosophy always served her very well. She had very little turnover and her tellers were always anxious to do what was asked and more.

The face of your office can be inviting and professional, or a turn-off. It is critical you find someone who has good interpersonal skills. So when you are purchasing your next cup of coffee at Starbucks® or McDonalds®, or an item at Target®, keep your eyes peeled for that exceptional person who goes out of their way to assist you, as that might be your next best employee.

Chapter 43

Can't Take Notes? One Tip on Efficient Note-Taking

"I Just Can't Take Good Notes"

We have all been there, the late evening doldrums or distractions that keep you from concentrating on a lecture or seminar which you know is important, but you just can't concentrate. You may be suffering from note-taking fatigue.

For several years, using an application called "Soundnote," I often leave meetings with a full recording of the conversation with cryptic notes attached. I don't have to take detailed notes because I record the entire conversation during a meeting through my iPad. I can go in later and listen to the recording and retrieve the part of the recorded conversation at the exact point where I typed any word. For instance, I could be halfway through the meeting and type the word "goals" at the point in the meeting that goals were discussed. If I click on the word "goals" on my written notes, the marker for the recording goes to 22:42 minutes in the conversation to hear the actual audio discussion at that point.

This app uses the recorder in my iPad and does a pretty commendable job of picking up conversations in the room, even if the speaker is some distance from me. It also allows me to type comments and write with a stylus or with my finger to do drawings or diagrams during the presentation.

This application, when open, looks like a page on a legal tablet. You can type into it just like into any note-taking app. You can also free-hand scroll on it with a smart pen, or you could do nothing but record the session. I find that I can concentrate on the conversation and need to only take periodic one- or two-word notes at critical times to mark the position of critical information that I might want to access later. There are a number of available apps that allow you to record information for recovery later, such as GoodNotes,

OneNote, Evernote, AudioNote, SuperNote, iAnnotate, and Notes Plus. Some of these are free and, of course, there are premium versions with additional features at an additional price.

For iOS, there are quite a few note-taking apps, including SuperNote, Evernote, Google Keep, Simple Note, Audio Note. And for Android, you can choose between Note Everything Pro, with text and voice that synchs with Google Docs. Also, you can download AK Notepad, Evernote, and AudioNote.

For a comparison of ten different apps in a single chart for multiple platforms, go to http://appcrawlr.com/app/uberGrid/403489, which offers a clear and concise summary of some of the better note-taking applications on the market.

All of these have great features, and none of them offer every feature on every platform. I would recommend you try them out before buying or try the free versions first to find out what best suits your particular needs. But for value, ease of use, and time, you can't beat SoundNote.

This app is only one of many that will free you up to do other things and help you be better organized. Unfortunately, at this time, SoundNote is only available for iOS and I have been using it on my iPad for about three years and it has never failed me yet. In addition, I like this app because I can share my recording and my notes with others as an email document without audio, or I can share it with the audio attached using Dropbox.

If you want an app that crosses over between iOS and Android platforms, you are going to be somewhat limited. As of my last search, I could only find two such applications—Evernote and AudioNote for Notepad and Voice Recorder. You can also save AudioNote as a .WAV file. Evernote gives you quite a bit of flexibility when you wish to share it across platforms and it has a free version that allows recording. That gives you greater flexibility to be able to use it on other platforms. For most users, crossing platforms is not a problem. If you save a document/recording in SoundNote on iOS, for instance, you can open it in other platforms as an MP3 or text document. It may not have all of the original functions, but you can always go back to the original platform to revive those features if necessary. Many people use Evernote, so it has pretty good accessibility for many users. It also has good handwriting recognition if you choose to use a stylus when taking notes.

Why more people don't use some of these apps mystifies me. Even using a recording app without written notes has potential to help you keep organized and allows you to capture tasks or information without taxing your memory. As you develop more contacts in practice and add files at different stages of maturity, it will become increasingly more difficult for you to keep track of your tasks without an ability to capture information on the road without some of these tools that were absent only ten years ago. I have a free app on my Android called Easy Voice Recorder, and I have used it for several years without fail. When I travel, I frequently open the app and periodically, I record items to be documented later. Some of my best ideas arise while I am driving long distances. That "down time" is productive time for me, but it would have much less value if I had not recorded some of the ideas that come to mind while driving. There is a "Pro" version of this app, which allows you to download to Google Drive. That feature gives you even greater flexibility in your planning and the ability to synchronize information captured in one format but available to share with others. Easy Voice and SoundNote are both very user friendly and I know I could function without them, but they certainly make it easier to be more efficient and productive.

If you want to be a hero during your next meeting, do an audio recording and send it to the chair or organizer of that meeting as an MP3, shared file on your Google Drive, or download it on a thumb drive for use later. I can tell you that I have done this many times to the surprise of the person who called the meeting. The better practice would be to tell the attendees that you will be recording the meeting for note-taking purposes. When sensitive matters are being discussed, recording the event may not be appropriate. The recording could also be offered with restricted access through your Google Drive, Dropbox or other sharing platform as well.

Good luck and happy note-taking!

Chapter 44

Google Scholar and Other Free Research Sources: Do You Still Need a Large Library for Legal Research?

Why Not Get It for Free?

It is surprising to me how many law students and solos are not familiar with Google Scholar. Although it has its limitations, it is very user friendly. It does not require password access and it includes many resources that you cannot access through Westlaw or Lexis.

From a cost-effective standpoint, it would seem that free legal research tools would always beat out a fee-based research database for legal research. Especially for the new solo establishing his or her practice, overhead must be a primary consideration.

If you are unfamiliar with Google Scholar, I highly recommend that you spend some time familiarizing yourself with it. In the 2014 ABA TechReport, Google Scholar, Casemaker, and Fastcase were listed as three of the most commonly accessed free resources.

As reported in that TechReport, research tools Casemaker and Fastcase were the clear winners among solo practitioners. Google Scholar was running a close second. This, I suspect was due to the priority placed on currency and accuracy for those two research tools giving the solo practitioner greater confidence in the result. Nevertheless, for other reasons, I believe you should not rule out Google Scholar, as it has been continuously improved since its introduction in 2003 and it offers features missing from other resources.

In 2014, the most frequently used free research tool at 38 percent was, to no one's surprise, Google. That was considerably less the case for solo practitioners (26 percent) than the largest firm practitioners (47 percent). Solos' preferred free research tool was a state Bar association offering (likely Casemaker or Fastcase) at 36 percent. Such tools were considerably less popular at the largest firms where just 6 percent of respondents chose them. That may be the result of large firms' common use of the pricier alternatives historically. It may be that they haven't made a transition, as habits die hard.

When establishing a solo practice, it would seem prudent to keep your expenditures as low as possible. So free would be my first choice.

Why would you pay for a service that you can obtain for free? My guess would be that many of the solos just have not been exposed to Google Scholar, Casemaker, or Fastcase the way that they are to Westlaw or Lexis during law school. For good reason, Westlaw and Lexis are viewed as more accurate and better professional resources than free resources by many of the legal research professors. They are provided at no charge to law students and, as a result, are more familiar and comfortable to use when first going solo. Also, the TechReport points out a higher satisfaction level among users of the fee-based services.

Regardless of brand, the results showed very clearly that while lawyers may turn to free research tools first, they're ultimately far more satisfied with fee-based tools. When asked to rate their satisfaction with various features of research tools, the following reported being "very satisfied" with the features of both free and fee-based tools:[1]

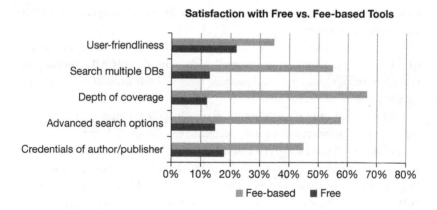

Satisfaction with Free vs. Fee-based Tools

---

1. American Bar Association, "ABA Legal Technology Survey Report 2014," http://www.americanbar.org/publications/techreport/2014/legal-research.html.

Although Google Scholar may have its drawbacks, as may be apparent from the graph, it has the most user-friendly interface in my opinion and may be the reason Westlaw and Lexis have modified their platforms. And you can find basic background information about the topic you are researching, which may reduce the time to access a fee-based resource. If your state Bar offers Casemaker or Fastcase, that could be the next step to refine and update the cases you may have identified on Google Scholar.

The State Bar of Michigan webpage describes Casemaker, which is the free legal resource that they make available to their members, as follow:

> The State Bar of Michigan has partnered with Casemaker to bring premium state and federal research materials to its membership. This service provides case law, constitution, and statutes for all 50 states, including the District of Columbia. In addition the service provides Michigan primary law, administrative code, state court rules, federal court rules, attorney general opinions, and the model civil jury instructions.[2]

Members also have access to several advanced legal research tools, including a case citation tool that simultaneously runs a search for secondary and/or third-party treatises and publications, and a tool capable of searching all customized books within any state and/or federal library in a single query.

In an effort to keep your overhead low, you might use online research options starting with Google Scholar, then switch to Casemaker or Fastcase (if offered as a member service for your state Bar). From there, you may be able to contact your law school reference librarian to follow up as necessary. Many law schools offer that service to their alums at no charge. There are many listservs associated with Bar associations where you can post queries after you have taken your research as far as you can. There you will often find some of the experts in the field responding with case references, forms, and other tips in advancing your clients' objectives that are not found in the books. And they do not charge for that assistance as a professional courtesy to other members of the Bar. Check them out and you will find that you are not alone as a solo anymore with all the resources available today online.

You might also want to take a look at http://guides.library.harvard.edu/free, where you can find an extensive list of free resources (not all without advertising). According to the website, these resources include Primary Federal Law, Primary State Law, Treaties, Foreign and International Law, Secondary Sources

---

2. https://www.michbar.org/opinions/opinionsearch.

and Legal Periodicals, and Empirical Sources of Information (data sets for the United States and the rest of the world). There are over thirty pages of resources referenced at that website. As with any research database, you are held accountable to ensure that the material resourced is accurate, up to date, and supported in the law. Because of the number of free resources, you can do your due diligence by cross-checking several free sources to see if there is consistency. Or you can use the free resources to get you where you believe you should be in the final analysis and go to a fee-based resource like Westlaw or Lexis to verify your result and, therefore, be billed for much less time for your usage on that platform.

However, now even Lexis is providing a free search website. I looked into this and found that it is (no surprise) not a full-service database that offers the same material as the paid version. Instead, it offers:

> The Lexis Web product includes important, legal-oriented Web content selected and validated by the LexisNexis editorial staff. You can trust that all content has met LexisNexis criteria for being authoritative and accurate. The current beta version combines content from thousands of Web sites and millions of Web pages, with more being added each day:
>
> - Governmental agency information (federal, state, local)
> - Informal commentary on legal issues (e.g., blogs specifically for lawyers and legal professionals)
> - General Web information about legal topics[3]

It appears that Lexis is trying to position itself to become the go-to resource for legal research, both free and fee based. When the rest of the world is giving away what you have traditionally charged others to access, then it may be time to compete by distinguishing your services into free and fee based with additional services such as more refined services or guarantees of accuracy that free services do not typically offer unless they are in concert with Bar membership or other paid memberships.

Ironically, the ABA's annual survey on technology and free resources is not free.

---

3. Simon Fadden, "LexisWeb," September 8, 2008, http://www.slaw.ca/2008/09/09/lexisweb.

Chapter 45

Disaster Preparedness: Your Duty and Obligation

Since most of you will be operating paperlessly using digital backup (hopefully I've convinced you), it is critical that you have a way to preserve that information in the event of a disaster. This chapter addresses some of the issues you may face and presents a plan of attack to prepare in the event of a disaster.

An article published in a 2013 issue of *Law Practice Today* points out a number of very important considerations when operating a law practice alone. The author states:

> According to the 2012 Legal Technology Survey Report, only 61 percent of respondents reported that their firm has such a plan. That number drops to 57 percent at small firms with two to nine attorneys and to just 50 percent among solo practitioners.[1]

The world is rife with disasters, from Hurricane Katrina–type natural disasters to the twin towers horrendous terrorist-inspired tragedy, all of which pose potential problems for the continuity of business operations for everyone. However, the local hot dog stand is not dependent on retention of a client list or holding critical confidential information which, when lost, may result in significant personal tragedy in addition to the fire, quake, hurricane, tornado, or other disaster befalling individuals.

Plus, as an attorney, you have a special obligation for business continuation under the Rules of Professional Conduct. It is not enough to say, "I will do my best to recover"; rather you need a plan to be in place.

---

1. Joshua Poje, "Preparing for a Disaster: Data Backup and Beyond," *Law Practice Today,* April 2013, http://www.americanbar.org/content/newsletter/publications/law_practice_today_home/lpt-archives/april13/preparing-for-a-disaster-data-backup-and-beyond.html.

With many attorneys operating in the cloud or fully digitized in a paper-less office, you have the added concern about protecting the security of that information. Although during Katrina it was clear that those attorneys who had data stored off-site were in far better shape than those attorneys who depended on paper files located in the path of that storm. Client personal information was fully disclosed to the elements in many instances.

In his piece, Poje recommends the following steps in preparedness.

First, analyze what you have currently stored and where it is located Is it in-house in physical form or partially or completely in the cloud? Does some of it reside in portable structures like portable hard-drives or thumb drives that are located in the office or in another location subject to the elements?

Second, he suggests to plan for backup with "two levels of redundancy." He describes both "data redundancy" and "geographic redundancy," meaning that digital copies of data need to be current and fully secure against possible threats of intrusion and that there should be more than one geographic location where it is preserved.

The third step Poje identifies is implementation of the plan.

This might seem as though Poje suggests the obvious, but in far too many instances this step is not undertaken because it is not seen as a priority. The exception to this step of the process may be observed in any firm that has suffered a fire, tornado, flood, or other occurrence in the past. I assure you that those firms have taken steps to do all three functions. This is not a profit-generating exercise—it is merely a risk-averse behavior that doesn't reach the managing partner's desk as rapidly as a drop in revenues.

The other problem is that you need "buy in" from everyone in the organization. As a solo practitioner that should not be a problem unless you fail to appreciate the risk and actually take time to build it into your business plan as an essential element for your success.

The fourth step Poje recommends is to test the system you have in place. This is also a critical step. You don't want to wait until disaster happens to find out that the system you have in place to back up your data is inaccessible or that it can't be retrieved in a form that you can readily use, or that it is missing entire critical and essential elements. Or it can't be retrieved because of an archaic storage system that no one uses anymore.

The final step Poje recommends is to review the system you have in place on a periodic basis to keep it up to date based on technological developments. That means that you will need to have a dynamic and regularly reviewed system in place. As a solo, that means that you will need to keep abreast of current developments in technology and storage/backup developments.

Ernest Svenson's 2006 article "Lessons from Katrina" is a good example of recovery from a natural disaster. In it, the author recounts how he dealt with that event and some recommendations for your own preparation.

Svenson explores how he had to relocate to Kansas City, then to Houston, and finally to Baton Rouge in an attempt to reestablish his practice. He tells how, "The destruction suffered by parts of the city created its own set of problems and exposed weaknesses both large and small. Storing information on paper turned out to be a particularly weak link." And he tells how paper systems in this scenario were not "safer" as compared to storing data in digital or other forms. You just can't take all that paper with you in the event of a disaster like Katrina, where there wasn't enough time to plan a move or, quite frankly, even to get out of New Orleans as the disaster enveloped the entire city and region. There was no place to go.

Even hauling out desktop computers and other equipment was not feasible in many instances. Roads were blocked, streets were flooded, and buildings were often potentially dangerous coffin-like containment structures as the water rose.

Svenson explored mobility in lawyering, but pointed out that having a laptop with all his files contained on the hard drive along with his smartphone for client contacts, allowed him to continue operations without severe interruptions. It also avoided a need to reconstruct all his files, which would put anyone out of business in short order.

One interesting side note that he pointed out was that he couldn't make cell phone calls, but he could text using his cell phone. He is a strong proponent of "web-based applications," which, in concert with Wi-Fi, allows one to maintain a link of communications with clients. He pointed out that Internet connection is and was critical for him. However, CloudLocker by Sto Amigo, mentioned earlier in this book, would not be affected by an inability to access files through web-based applications—one of the reasons I discussed it as an option.

He also pointed out how the firm that he worked for had an internal email system and was not using Gmail. But since his personal account was a Gmail account, he could continue to send and receive emails without interruption.

One observation that Svenson made concerned using in-house servers that are not backed up in the cloud or elsewhere where they might be able to be retrieved in the event the geographic redundancy mentioned above is missing. As he explained,

Another area that caused major problems for my law firm after Katrina was getting our billing system to work again. Because the system was run from servers located in the New Orleans office, our offices in Baton Rouge, Lafayette, and Houston also were unable to send out bills or enter time. The law firm finally hired a company to go into the city, remove the servers from the main office on the 40th floor, and set them up in another city. This task took almost two weeks and was nerve-wracking for all concerned—as well as costly.[2]

Ultimately, he decided to go solo himself and used a system that was hosted in the cloud.

He is a strong proponent of scanning documents and explains that at first it seemed intimidating to scan documents, but that over time he has become accustomed to that process and that it is easy to do.

Bottom line: go digital, scan, backup in the cloud, and you can operate without serious interruption in the event of a natural disaster.

He has two well-known legal blogs: www.ernietheattorney.net and pdfforlawyers.com which you may want to visit.

---

2. Ernest Svenson, "Lessons from Katrina," *GPSolo magazine,* December 2006, http://www.americanbar.org/content/newsletter/publications/gp_solo_magazine_home/gp_solo_magazine_index/lessonsfromkatrina.html.

Chapter 46

How Should I Organize My Business?

There are a number of ways to organize yourself as a business organization and, since you will be in charge, you get to decide. As you make your decision, you need to consider protection from liability, transferability, and flexibility of ownership; and income tax and estate tax implications as you make your choice.

Sole Proprietor

This is the simplest and easiest way to start out in business formation as you are operating the business as YOU. You don't need to file taxes separately, you don't need to identify yourself as a specific type of business entity, and everything is as before, except you are now Gary Bauer, Attorney at Law on your stationery, to your clients and to the state and federal government, and that is it. You may want to register an assumed name so that you can operate under that name in business in your state and so that others can find you under that name as connected to it.

But as you expand your practice and take on responsibility for more and more cases and start earning greater sums of money, it might make sense to insulate yourself from personal liability and reform your organization to take greater advantage of the tax laws or the ability to maintain continuity of the business in the event something happens to you. In that case, a different vehicle for business formation might be in order.

Partnership

You could decide to join forces with someone else and form a partnership. I have known students who decided to form partnerships with their former study partners in law school. Some have worked out, some have not. The reasons for joining forces such as sharing the overhead, collaborating on cases, expanding your marketing presence, specializing in a greater number of areas of law with each of you providing services that the other still does not, are reasons I often hear students recite for that type of business format. Frankly, it also allows you to have coverage for hearings in the event you are not able to be present and to take over in the event of a catastrophe where you cannot return to work. All of that still doesn't justify putting the risk of success or failure in the hands of another and forming a partnership right out of law school.

My response to those students who are considering a partnership is to ask them why they couldn't gain the same benefits by simply sharing office space. An office mate can share expenses, cover hearings, collaborate on cases, and share ideas. You just don't share the risk. But what risk?

Short of marketing for both firms, there is really nothing that you can't do except share the income. You can even have a contingency plan for takeover in the event one of you is disabled or killed in an accident.

And there is a big downside to being partners with your classmate: unless you have been lifelong friends, it is unlikely you will know them well enough to risk running a business together and have to depend on them for your income. You and your best friend in law school might have great times together socially. You might find that you are compatible study mates. However, the first day you are in your new office working late one Friday afternoon completing a brief that is due the following week while your partner has taken the afternoon off to play a round of golf with his buddies, you may have misgivings about joining him in a business venture. What if you feel you want to purchase computers that are Apple computers, yet your partner wants PCs instead? What if you can't agree on an advertising budget or how much to keep as retained earnings versus wages paid to each partner?

And the truth is that divorces can be ugly. This is particularly true with law firm splitups. Who keeps which client files? How are all the assets divided? If you can't agree in dissolution, it may end up in litigation. That is not the kind of public spectacle that you want your competition to parlay to their advantage.

Conversely, if you share office space for a year and find that you are compatible as far as business administration, ethics, family values, and long-term goals, then you can always form a partnership or other business entity in which you join forces and chances are that you will not lose any competitive advantage by doing so. In fact, it may actually work to your advantage to send out announcements and have an open house to celebrate the event.

Professional Limited Liability Corporation

First, the traditional corporation structure and an LLC are different in the eyes of the IRS and very different in tax treatment and administrative requirements. Most solos will not need to be established under that type of structure. Since the sole proprietorship is so simple, many new solos default into that status and just "hang a shingle" in their name and begin to offer their services without the necessity of anything more than that.

But as your business grows and potential liability increases with every case that you open, you may look for cover so that you are protecting your personal assets from claims of malpractice by your clients. But many state rules of professional conduct do not allow you to shield yourself from liability by simply forming a corporate structure. Also, when you first start out, if you do business with another business, like a bank, they are going to ask for personal guarantees if you have a Professional Limited Liability Corporation (PLLC) before giving you a loan so that the protection you are seeking will not be against those entities either.

Probably the most popular business organization format for most solo practitioners is the PLLC. (Some differences occur in some states, but the majority of states require the formation of a PLLC if you are a licensed professional. Check with your state for which format is authorized or required for you.) If a PLLC is set up and maintained properly, this can protect your personal assets in the event of malpractice. That doesn't mean you can't be sued or held accountable for malpractice; it only protects your personal assets from seizure or other claims. Your business assets in the PLLC would be subject to claims by those creditors.

Unlike a traditional corporation business structure, a PLLC allows you to treat the business income as personal income and only be taxed on that income once. In a traditional corporation, the income of the firm is taxed and then again when wages are paid to the members or dividends paid to the shareholders. So that income is taxed twice. In an effort to enhance small business development, the IRS, along with legislation in all the states, now authorize LLCs. The LLC is a relatively new development and in 1977, Wyoming was the first state to pass legislation allowing LLCs to be chartered under that state's laws.

LLCs have all the advantages of a corporation structure for the small business owner with few of the negative attributes. And as long as the structural and administrative requirements are adhered to, it will afford the owner protection against his or her personal assets. By far, that is the greatest concern for most solos. That doesn't mean you should not carry malpractice insurance— quite the opposite. As mentioned above, this structure doesn't protect you from liability as to your business assets.

Limited Partnerships/"S" Status LLC/Corps and Other Matters

There are other business structures that you can establish, such as Limited Partnerships or "S" status LLCs or Corporations. These are beyond the scope of this book, as the majority of you will chose the sole proprietorship, partnership, or PLLC when you first start up. My advice is that you find a good accountant or CPA and ask them about how you should structure your firm, given your state laws and your long-term goals for your business. You may also want to consult with other solos in your area to ask them how they structured their business and why that might or might not be the best approach for you. Many of them will have already struggled with that issue and over time, they will have had to deal with their decision with various outcomes that might be good or bad. Ask them and learn from them as well. Then you decide what is best for you.

Chapter 47

Malpractice Insurance

No discussion about formation of a law practice would be complete without discussion of malpractice insurance. This is not where you want to scrimp and save money. Again, saving money should be your second priority whereas MAKING MONEY should be your first priority. Do not start your practice uninsured. When you first start out, you will find that the rates are reasonable because you are a low-risk client. The reason is that you have so few cases and clients that the insurer has very little risk underwriting your work. But as your practice matures you will find that your rates will go up. But then you will be making more money anyway, right?

What kind of coverage do you need and how much will it cost? There are two major types of policies.

- **Claims Made Policies:** Policies that cover you for claims made when the policy was in force. For instance, you have a policy in force and covering you only for the calendar year 2016; you do not have that policy before or after that calendar year. Any claim made during that calendar year is covered, but a claim made because of a mistake during 2016 that was made in 2017 would not be covered even though you were covered and made the mistake in 2016. This type of policy should motivate you to make the claim as soon as possible during the policy period.
- **Occurrence Policies:** Policies that cover you for a claim that arose when the policy was in force. For instance, you have a policy that was in force in calendar year 2016 and the act that was the basis for the claim occurred in 2016, but the claim wasn't made until 2017 when you no longer had a policy in force. An occurrence policy would cover that claim. This type of policy doesn't depend on your prompt reporting to stay within the covered period. (That doesn't mean you shouldn't report a claim promptly.)

Other terms you might hear when shopping for a policy might include "tail" coverage. What this covers is "notice of circumstance" language that allows you to be covered as long as you give the insurer notice of circumstances, which might give rise to a potential claim that you believe might ripen into an actual claim later. And if you comply, you would be covered by that insurance provider even if you no longer have coverage under that carrier. You should look for this in your policy coverage.

What if you were not on notice of prior circumstances and you are being insured by a new insurer? Would that insurer want to have liability for past activities? How might you cover yourself for claims based on your actions under a now expired policy? This is called "tail" coverage, which you can obtain from your current carrier to cover you even after the policy period has expired. This protects a new insurer from liability for your past acts while insured by someone else. In other words, you can pay for extended reporting protection from your current insurer.

Price

Price can vary quite a bit depending on your area of practice, how many areas of practice you undertake, how much coverage you wish to have, and how the policy is written. If you want a figure, OK, I will give you one: $500 a year. The problem with that number is that all the variables I just mentioned can make it higher or lower. I guarantee you can get coverage for that amount, but with what terms? See my point?

When shopping for insurance, I would recommend that you use a broker to get you the best price with the best terms. Check your local Bar journal or Google brokers in your area and use them to become better educated and to get your best price. This is one area where another solo might not be your best source of information as they have probably established providers and once in place are reluctant to change or to see it as a priority to shop for the best bargain. Brokers, by contrast, will be up to date on what providers are doing and what kind of pricing is most competitive.

Chapter 48

Student Debt Management

You have graduated from law school, passed the Bar, and want to go solo. But you have $100,000 in student loans, which are coming due. How can you start your business unless you are able to keep up with your student loan payments?

There are a number of programs for student loan forgiveness, forbearance, deferral, or consolidation of loan payments.

Income-Driven Plans

For federal student loans this means that a person can have an income-driven payment plan that offers repayment at 10 to 20 percent of your discretionary income depending on which program you are eligible for. But remember: we no longer have "debtor prisons" and if your cash flow is delayed at the inception of your practice, you have some relief in the form of reduced payments. According to the U.S. Department of Education, "Depending on your income and family size, you may have no monthly payment at all."[1]

But, even though that reduction gives you relief, it doesn't mean that interest stops accruing so, pay as much as you can as soon as you can to pay off those loans as soon as possible.

Loan Forgiveness

Conversely, you may qualify for Public Service Loan Forgiveness (PSLF).

Qualifying employment for the PSLF program is not about the specific job that you do for your employer. Rather, it is about who your employer is.

---

1. https://studentaid.ed.gov/sa/repay-loans/understand/plans/income-driven.

Employment with the following types of organizations qualifies for PSLF:

- Government organizations at any level (federal, state, local, or tribal)
- Not-for-profit organizations that are tax-exempt under Section 501(c)(3) of the Internal Revenue Code
- Other types of not-for-profit organizations that provide certain types of qualifying public services
- Serving in a full-time AmeriCorps or Peace Corps position also counts as qualifying employment for the PSLF Program.[2]

For most federal student loans there is a grace period of six months after graduation, which can be extended for up to three years under certain circumstances before you even have to start repayment. Again, of course, interest continues to accrue during that time period.

Loan Forbearance

According to the National Consumer Law Center's Student Loan Borrower Assistance Project:

> Grace periods can be extended for up to three years (in addition to the standard six months) if a borrower is serving on active duty in the Armed Forces. Repayment begins after the grace period is over. You can only use the grace period once per loan, so if you go back to school after your grace period ends, that loan will not be eligible for a second grace period upon graduation from the subsequent program. New loans will be eligible for a grace period.[3]

You have the ability to schedule your repayment in a manner that you can afford. If you keep your expenses low and stick to your business plan, you should see a steady stream of income to begin repayment as soon as possible. Keep your lenders fully informed regarding your financial status in the event you have programs which adjust your payments based upon your discretionary income and, if possible, prepay to keep your interest charges at the

---

2. https://studentaid.ed.gov/sa/repay-loans/forgiveness-cancellation/public-service.
3. http://www.studentloanborrowerassistance.org/repayment/postponing-repayment/grace-periods.

minimum. Look at all your payments and pay off the highest interest rate loans first, if at all possible.

I have several students who have graduated and have been able to pay off their student loans in three or four years because of their success in solo practice. Not everyone will be that successful, but it can be done and as a solo, there are no limits to how much you can earn. That cannot be said of employment with others, for the most part.

Part V

Client Control Issues

Chapter 49

Litigation: Is That the Answer for Your Clients?

Don't think there are no crocodiles because the water is calm.

Malayan Proverb

Most students graduate from law school without significant experience in the courtroom. Many of their classes have been taught using the Socratic method with appellate cases as the basis for those discussions (some would say confrontations) in class. Professors use this method to help the students to understand the analysis and the logic employed by the justices to support their final opinions.

So, throughout law school, students are engaged in animated discussions in class. Upon graduation, they may feel the urge to demonstrate their legal prowess. And, in my experience, many of them tend to be geared toward litigation, rather than mediation or reconciliation, as they engage other lawyers in the resolution of their client's legal issue. And many clients feel that litigation is most likely to produce the outcome they desire.

But Litigation Is Risky

The reality is that anytime you litigate a matter and depend on a judge or jury to determine the outcome, it is like playing the lottery. I say this because on any given day a judge can rule against you. You can make a record for an appeal later. But if your client doesn't have the means to pursue an appeal, it may not be the law, but it is the law to you!

Juries fill out questionnaires and you hope to pick jurors based on that information coupled with your voir dire. But the truth is, there is far more information about their lives that you cannot access, which is buried deep in their conscious or subconscious. This can affect the outcome of the case in ways that you never anticipated. And this increases the risk that the outcome may not be the one you or your client anticipated.

Set Realistic Expectations

As you counsel your client, you must keep this in mind: do not guarantee results or suggest a definite outcome. Although this should be fairly obvious, sometimes it is only learned the hard way. It may not be obvious, but many times your comments may create false impressions in your client's mind setting the stage for unrealistic expectations regarding the outcome. Be careful how you frame the possible outcomes when litigation is at play. This is one of the major reasons, in my opinion, why lawyers have such a poor reputation among so many in the general population. It is easy to give the impression that a client's cause of action has greater merit than is justified. As you are trying to impress your clients with your abilities to close the sale, they may put more weight on the positive outcomes than they should. But often they have adopted those attitudes only from the way you portrayed the possible outcomes.

Lesson number 1: underpromise and overdeliver. This means that you must set realistic expectations when counseling a client and caution him or her that there cannot be guarantees when there are unpredictable variables; and in litigation, there are always unpredictable variables.

Lesson number 2: don't make the client your friend. When I was in sales, I was told never to make dealers my friends. Be friendly toward them, establish relationships with them, but don't make them your friends. The minute dealers sell a piece of equipment out of trust and you arrive to find it missing without payment to the wholesaler, you are put in a position of taking them to task to pay for the equipment or reporting them to your superiors. If you are their "friend" they will ask you to "cover the shortage until they can make it right." You are in a business relationship, not a personal relationship; keep it that way. That doesn't mean you can't have lunch together, but don't put yourself in the position of being their child's godfather unless, of course, you are related. (That is another story.)

Lesson number 3: don't make the client's problems your problems. Often a client will come to you with a problem that has a resolution that requires you to engage in activity that is criminal or would require you to violate the code of ethics. Your client is in terrible trouble and to resolve it without violations of the law or ethics could be costly and time consuming. They implores you to solve their problem but in doing so, you make their problem your problem. Don't do it. Send them to your worst enemy but don't be tempted to take on a mantle of guilt because you didn't follow a path to your potential professional self-destruction.

Lesson number 4: don't subject yourself to abuse by your clients. When you are in solo practice, you are dependent on your clients to pay their bills. As an attorney, you do not have to suffer abuse at the hands of your client. "Pull the choke-chain" like you would to train a bad dog, figuratively, anytime your clients treat you with disrespect. Get their attention early on and tell them that you will not tolerate them raising their voice or using profanity when speaking with you. Tell them that no one in your private life nor anyone in your professional life can treat you with disrespect. If they are looking for someone to abuse, it will have to be someone else and show them the door. That will make the point and the word will get out that you are a consummate professional, that you treat others that way, and that you expect to be treated in a similar manner. Start early and always be conscious of your behavior around others, whether in a professional or casual setting. This will pay dividends over the life of your career.

Lesson number 5: lose the "dead wood" before it becomes a drain on your resources. You may feel that if you don't instill confidence, the client will go elsewhere. But you are better served losing a potential client who is controlling and demanding than to make their problem your problem. I have heard it said that "20 percent of your clients will take 80 percent of your time and the ones who say it is about the 'principle' are often the ones who won't pay when the 'principal' comes due." Many of the solos I have interviewed tell me that it often takes years to finally learn to be discriminating and turn away potential clients who ultimately turn out to be the most demanding and most difficult when it comes to collections.

But, in reality, mediation offers many clients the best recourse to solve their problems; they just don't understand this.

Mediation May Be the Best Answer

If you look up *Trial Lawyer Magazine* for July 1988 (I believe that was the issue), you will find an article titled "Client's Perceptions of Litigation," which has excellent content and demonstrates why mediation is often a better means of resolving conflict for a client than litigation.

One example posed in that article concerned a woman stopped by a police officer for speeding. She disputed the charge and told the officer that she definitely was not speeding. But he cited her despite her protestations. She fought the ticket and asked for a hearing. On the day set for the hearing the officer failed to show. As a result, the judge dismissed the charges and excused her from the courtroom. But she objected and asked to be allowed to give testimony. The judge said, "Ma'am, perhaps you don't understand, you won! The charges are dismissed." She replied, "But, your honor, I want to have my day in court and tell you why I was wronged."

Whose Day in Court Is It?

Clients want to have their day in court and tell their story—but that usually isn't what happens. In the courtroom, the client is often very frustrated with the process. When conducting direct examination of your client, the client will have to answer the questions that you think are important. On cross, they have to follow the agenda of opposing counsel who challenges their honesty and cuts them off when they have more to say. But they can't say what they would like to say.

Even as you sit at counsel table during the testimony of witnesses, you will find your client will want to communicate with you concerning the veracity of that testimony or significance of that record. All of this occurs while you are trying to concentrate on that witness' testimony. You silence your client as you try to listen intensively. The result is a frustrated client, regardless of the outcome. (Hint: give them a notepad and pen and tell them to take good notes. Tell them that you will look at those notes before excusing the witness to do follow-up as necessary. This keeps them occupied and allows you to listen without interruptions.)

It Is the Emotional Capital They Don't Want to Spend

Lawyers often experience a client's change of heart on the courthouse steps just prior to trial. To prep your client, you will put them through anticipated questions they may face on cross-examination during trial. You do this to help them understand what they will experience as opposing counsel will critically prod and probe every word of their testimony. During this process, they begins to understand that the emotional capital that they have to expend is often perceived as too much to bear and they wants to back out and just make it all go away. Then in order to make it go away, they agrees to settle for terms that they thought they would never surrender to and you are viewed as the villain because they didn't get what they wanted originally as the outcome.

Mediation May Be the Solution

Mediation, by contrast, starts by giving both participants an opportunity, without interruption, to do what they have been wanting to do all along. They get to tell their story in the presence of a referee, of sorts, to the other side. The other person who has not listened to them before must listen to them vent their anger. This allows them to drop a huge amount of pent up emotional expression to the one who has, in their view, wronged them. All of this occurs in a controlled environment. Most of the time that has been their goal all along.

The next step in the process is one in which the participants negotiate a solution. The resolution is one that they are empowered to create with the help of the mediator. It is a solution that usually means that neither one gets everything they want. But they often accept it and can live with that resolution because it is one that they own and they created. This is ideal, particularly when there is a continuing relationship between the parties that, of necessity, must continue. For instance, neighbors disputing boundary lines will continue to live next to one another as neighbors.

The solution that they create is one that they will enforce if it is one of their making. A resolution that is determined after litigation through a court order will be one that is followed according to the letter of the law, but may not be followed in the spirit of the law. The neighbor who lost the lot line dispute may play his radio at increased volume at all hours of the night and still respect the new court-ordered boundary line. So mediation offers an opportunity for the neighbors to make amends through the mediation process and move on from there. So too, in the case of divorces, mediation can allow the parties to communicate effectively and resolve their conflicts in a manner that will allow them to express their grievances and manage their affairs without the constant and subsequent intervention of the courts to enforce an order that they do not want to honor.

Mediation may not be appropriate under certain circumstances. When physical or sexual abuse has transpired, or if it is necessary to establish a legal precedent, mediation may not be in order. But far too many conflicts are resolved in the courtroom that may have been played out with better results for the participants in mediation. In the end, the perception by the client of the attorney's value to them may be enhanced when mediation is employed. Always give it consideration before going to trial and you may find greater success attracting and retaining new clients.

Chapter 50

Barriers to Communication: Learn to Listen Effectively

Don't talk unless you can improve the silence.

Jorge Luis Borges

One very dramatic method I use to train my students to be more effective communicators was shared with me early on in my teaching career. It consists of two sets of blocks.

My students counsel live clients and prepare their estate planning documents. If they were to approach that task like many attorneys do, they would have a checklist of items to be completed. Clients must follow their attorney's agenda answering inquiries like, "Are you married?," "Do you have any children?," and "What are their ages?" and so forth until the questionnaire is completed.

During the entire interview, the client is dying to tell the attorney about the disastrous process she experienced when her mother died and how the family fought over every little detail of distribution. She wants the attorney to know how two of her siblings will no longer speak to one another. The client wants to make sure that her plan will avoid that problem if at all possible.

But the attorney never heard about her concerns because it wasn't on his checklist.

The client departs and returns to finalize her documents later. The attorney presents those documents in a nice, simulated leather binder, and they part company. The client will never return for future services. Nor will that client ever refer others to that attorney. But why?

It is because the attorney's agenda didn't allow the client to express herself and talk about what she felt was important. In fact, the client didn't really understand why her feelings about her earlier experience were never heard.

She thought certain information was important, but he is an experienced attorney. Who is she to question the process? Apparently that information wasn't legally significant or the attorney would have asked questions that would have allowed her to explore it. The truth is that the attorney never connected with the client and never got to the root of the problem or established a relationship with that client. She will never be heard from again.

The attorney who "processes" clients, produces their documents, and sends them out the door is, in my opinion, all too common. Such attorneys can be found everywhere. You must learn to connect with your client. It is about establishing relationships. But that cannot be accomplished using the checklist approach, following your agenda, and not the client's. The only way to find out what the client's agenda is is to allow the client to set the stage and paint the picture that he wishes to paint. If you "process" your client's information using the "checklist approach," you will be competing with online resources. Because that is what online resources do. They process forms based on pre-canned inquiries. They use the "if—then" modality. There is no opportunity for the online applicant to express themselves beyond the format provided. You are not a computer; don't act like one! If you act like a computer, expect to get paid an equivalent amount for your services.

The Blocks

To help my students better understand the point I wish to make, I select two volunteers. Each one takes one set of blocks. One of them is directed to build something with the blocks so that they are all touching one another. Upon completion of that task, I instruct the other student to reproduce that configuration while sitting next to the first student in view of her assembly. Of course, he replicates it without difficulty and I ask the rest of the students to give him a "hand" for his fine work.

Next, they are instructed to take a position with their backs to one another so that they cannot view what the other is doing. I tell one of them to reassemble the blocks in another pattern once again. Once that is done, I tell the student with the unassembled blocks to reproduce what the other student just created using "leading questions" only. In other words, the answer by the other student must be "yes" or "no" or, if fifteen seconds elapse (as nonresponsive), to ask another leading question in an attempt to recreate what that student has assembled. This leads to a great deal of frustration as the blocks consist of three different wedges, two different squared blocks, and two different cylinders. Try this yourself using Legos® or two sets of identical items.

The blocks I use can't be distinguished by color. Calling something a "wedge" is inadequate to distinguish one wedge from another. Also, the position of each block creates even greater issues of identification. The orientation as to which side is grounded must be described with surgical precision, and how the position of one to the other can be appropriately described is even more frustrating. They struggle, but eventually the "assembler" will complete the task. I then ask them to view one another's assembly.

After thirteen years of using this three times a year, not once has a student completed this project with any degree of success. It tells them, "Your clients have a picture in their mind that you will need to replicate to address their goals completely." Your clients' picture is their agenda, not yours. However, the client has an infinite number of blocks to build upon. And, unlike this exercise, NONE of their blocks are identical to yours. Yet if you attempt to construct their "assembly" by asking leading questions and forcing them to follow your agenda, you will never match their "picture."

What is their agenda?

You need to ask open-ended questions such as, "Tell me about yourself," "What brought you here today?" "Tell me about your family." "Tell me about your experiences concerning the transfer of property upon someone's death in your family." Ask them about the dynamics of the relationships among their children. What are they attempting to accomplish with their estate plan? What are their most important objectives in passing their property?

Ask them for background and context. What experiences have they had with probate? If you allow them to talk about it, you will be better able to draft documents that address the issues they feel are important based on their own experiences. Most of the time you will find that your agenda will be accomplished and the items on your checklist will be answered as the clients' conversations will often contain the information you seek. They will describe their family, how many children they have, their marital status, and so forth. Follow-up and prompt them to explore in more detail certain information that you will need such as, "How old are your children?" But allow them to lead the conversation and you become the follower. Listen more, talk less.

Tell Me About Yourself

Why do some practices grow while others struggle to survive? Largely, it is a function of good communication. That means that you must CONNECT with your client. Relationship building is what it is about and you cannot create a relationship unless you understand what is important to that client. It is the only thing that will distinguish you from your competitors.

How do you connect? Find something that triggers a response that tells you the client is engaged. You will know it when you see it. Ask them to "Tell me about yourself." Try to find points of connection between you and your client. For instance, they might tell you that they served in the military. If true, you could add that so did your father during World War II. Oh, and they were both in the Air Force. Build on the similarities and connectors. Once you make a connection, and continue to make more connections, they will become more forthcoming and willing to talk to you about what is important to them. You will build trust as they begins to see you more like them than before you engaged them. We all have connectors. Find those connectors between you and your client and you will become someone special, not just a lawyer drafting their estate plans. They will leave feeling good about you as someone who is truly concerned about what matters most to them. That is how you build trust and build return and referral business.

Chapter 51

Client Honesty: Don't Let the Client's Problem Become Your Problem

A True Story

A number of years ago while I was working as a regional sales manager for a Japanese company, it was necessary for me to travel extensively, often exceeding 100,000 miles a year on the road. I wore out a great number of vehicles. In 1979, while driving a brand new Buick Century on one of my calls, the radio quit working. Since it was under warranty, I took it to the nearest dealer for a repair.

At that time, credit cards were not being used as much as they are today. You couldn't charge your meal at a drive-thru like you can today. So it was necessary to carry a lot of cash on me. Waving too much money around was a major concern. Hiding money in a place that would allow me to access funds without carrying large sums of cash in my wallet necessitated covert action. The Buick Century had a fuse panel on the lower surface of the dash and could be easily removed. Four one hundred dollar bills fit neatly within that compartment where no one would ever discover it, so I thought.

Back to the repairs at the Buick dealership. I was told to wait in the customer lounge while a mechanic made the necessary repairs provided under warranty. Within a short period of time I was paged, the repair had been made. It was only a blown fuse. There was no charge for the repair. So once again, I was on my way. About ten miles down the road, it hit me! A fuse! Checking under the panel where the money was hidden revealed only fuses.

Now what? Call the police and have them investigate? It was my word against the mechanic's. What proof did I have that there was money in there in the first place? Back at the dealership the owner listened to my concerns and expressed serious doubt that his mechanic could be a thief. We met the mechanic who did the repairs. He denied seeing any money under that panel.

This was a very expensive lesson for me. I didn't have the time to fool around contacting the sheriff to seek a warrant for this man's arrest. Besides, the mechanic seemed shaken and nervous about the turn of events. And I really didn't want to get the mechanic in trouble; I just wanted my money returned. That is when I got an idea.

I said, "Perhaps the money slipped down below that panel where we couldn't see it. Would it be possible for you to remove the lower panel and check it out?" In the meantime, the owner and I could go up front and get a cup of coffee while we waited. Soon the mechanic came to the lounge and said, "I found it! Just as you suspected, the money had slipped below the panel and here it is." I thanked him for his assistance and never placed money in that location again. I also learned a valuable lesson about allowing someone to save face.

It wasn't that he was a bad person. The temptation was just too much. And when confronted, he felt the pangs of guilt and regret and the possible serious consequences of discovery. I found a way to allow him to walk through the door that gave him permission to undo the damage and save face. It was a win for both of us. Afterward, I investigated further and found there was no way for the money to slip below the fuse box due to the design of that panel. Had the sheriff been called, it could have had serious repercussions in that mechanic's life. I didn't want that.

In practice, it is often easier for a client to omit some of the negative facts of their case than to reveal them. They might do this to avoid embarrassment, or they might hope that those bad facts will never come to light during the litigation. As an experienced trial attorney, I can tell you that they will come out and at the worst possible time. Help your clients to full candor by telling them about the negative consequences of concealing the bad facts. You can tell them you have heard it all and that you need the complete story to defend them or prosecute their case. Tell them, "Don't tie my hands behind my back when I am trying to defend you."

You only need to be blind-sided once before this approach becomes your standard approach. The one thing you may not be able to predict, however, is how your client will present herself/himself at trial. As much as I work to prep my clients, I am always surprised by how willing they are to take it upon themselves to change the order of trial preparation and "wing it" with a new strategy of their own while on the stand. I often tell clients that anytime you go to trial, it is a crapshoot. On any given day, a judge or juror may respond in ways that are unimaginable and turn a sure winner into a loser.

But what you can try to control is full disclosure by the clients before going to trial. Help them to reveal the good, the bad, and the ugly by giving them permission to be human and disclose those facts. Emphasize the fact that we all do things that we may not wish to disclose. But remind them that hiding those facts from their attorney is not the position that they want to be in when the verdict is read.

Chapter 52

Cow in the House? Malpractice? Fess Up

Don't hide from your mistakes, confront them.

A True Story

A number of years ago someone called our office concerned about an elderly gent who was facing the possibility of losing his land due to a foreclosure. He asked that we send someone to where this man lived to see if there was a way to help him. It was in the dead of winter and very cold, with snow blowing everywhere. The property was in a rural area and the entire eighty acres were fenced so that cattle that grazed on that land could utilize every inch for pasture. Most fields are fenced so the cattle can graze the pasture areas, but this was unusual as the house was included in the area where the cattle roamed.

To approach the front door, I had to climb a gate and literally walk through a herd of about thirty Black Angus cattle to get to the front door. Most of those cattle were gathered around the front porch. The house was weathered and in serious disrepair. A screen door was hanging from one hinge in front of the entry door. I knocked on the door. As I waited, I heard someone moving around inside, so I waited and knocked again. Finally, after some time, an elderly gentleman answered the door and asked what I wanted.

After I had explained the purpose of my visit, he told me that it was true that someone was trying to take his farm from him. He told me that he couldn't keep up with the payments because he had to feed his cattle. As we spoke, a kerosene heater he had placed next to the couch provided a small amount of heat. We discussed whether he had heat and he invited me to touch a radiator against the wall. Touching it, I found that it was barely warm. It was apparent he was just getting by. He explained that the cattle were like pets to him and he didn't have the heart to take them to market.

As we sat on the couch, my attention was suddenly drawn to a very large dog that came into view in the room right next to where we were sitting. I am not afraid of dogs generally, but this "dog" was huge. As I did a double take, the farmer explained, "That is Daisy." Daisy was a cow!

As we talked, Daisy decided it was time to relieve herself and proceeded to urinate where she was standing while calmly chewing her cud. At that moment, the farmer said, "Now Daisy, I told you not to do that in here! Daisy, stop that right now!" as the cow continued to urinate without hesitation. The farmer seemed embarrassed and said she was in the house because she was young and it was cold outside.

As I was leaving, I observed a number of places on the carpet that appeared to be wet and circular in form. The delay answering the door may have been due to his attempts to clean up other debris so that it wasn't there when I came in.

Another True Story

A few years ago, one of my former students called me and said, "I think I committed malpractice!" She went on to explain the issue and her mistake and told me that it would probably cost the client $8,000 to rectify the situation. "What should I do?" she asked. I told her first to contact her malpractice insurance carrier and report the incident. Then to follow their instructions. I explained that they will most likely tell her to tell the client the truth (or expose the "cow") and to see what it will take to undo the damage.

She did as I told her and reported back to me several weeks later. The client told her not to worry about the oversight as she had done several months' worth of work for them prior to that problem arising, and they felt that that work had saved them substantially more already. Often our fears are unfounded and it is not an option to hide your missteps. Carry malpractice insurance, do the best work you can for your clients, and if you make a mistake, disclose it but only after contacting your insurance carrier, and learn from your mistake. You will not be the first lawyer to call a malpractice insurance carrier. But don't risk losing your license by trying to hide the "cow." It isn't worth it.

Chapter 53

The World Is Pass/Fail

Your reputation can be made after much hard work, or lost in an instant with little effort.

A friend of mine recently commented that we are so accustomed to evaluations in school represented by grades that it doesn't always register, until after graduation, that in the real world we either make the grade or don't. In other words, the world is pass/fail and not a report card grade that we can share with others. It is a black-and-white world in terms of the ultimate outcome.

On occasion, students ask me how many pages a report needs to be to get a good grade. Or a what is the minimum they need to do to get a passing grade. I tell them that that should not be their measure of success. They should strive to do their best no matter what the outcome.

The greater danger for most of us lies not in setting our aim too high and falling short, but in setting our aim too low, and achieving our mark.

Michelangelo

Chapter 54

Is Your Client a Twenty Footer? A Hard Lesson to Learn: When to Turn Away Business

"Well, it looked good at twenty feet. . . ."

A True Story

Last fall I participated in an auto auction in which over 2,000 antique and classic cars were sent through the auction. It was one of those national auctions that are televised. And some of the cars that go through the auction are incredible. It can be a great way to buy a car, but "buyer, beware!" I would always employ a professional to help guide me.

About twenty cars at a time are moved to a staging area in anticipation of moving them into an arena and onto a turntable where they are auctioned off. I was one of the drivers who would, upon command, start my chosen vehicle. After testing the brakes, I would drive it into one of the two elevated turntables to be auctioned off. So it was critical that I could stop the car lest it become embedded in the audience below. Once on the turntable, we were instructed to turn the engine off and wait as the auctioneer plied his powers of persuasion to foster a contest between two speculators turned buyers.

Being new to this driving experience, I found it to be quite a challenge as each of the cars or trucks had quite different characteristics. Some were "sticks," some were "automatics." Some were quite new and exotic with "paddle shifters." It was critical to find neutral and reverse to navigate safely to the stage, through a sizable crowd, and park each car after the gavel struck wood. After the cars took their turn on the turntable, we were instructed to wait as "pushers" would approach the vehicle from the rear and push it off stage down a ramp where we waited for a golf cart to lead us to the parking area.

As I sat in different cars or trucks in the staging area, potential buyers and kibitzers would come by and inspect the vehicles. Some would ask me to start them up to hear them run. "How many turns on the odometer?" Others would take magnets and flashlights checking for "bondo" (fiberglass filling rusted areas) or ripples in the metal indicating inferior or amateur restoration techniques.

Soon, I picked a late model Porsche 911 convertible to drive into the arena. As a novice, I had picked this as one of the more exotic and desirable cars. Soon a potential purchaser walked up to the car and checked it out. After some time, I asked him what he thought of the car. He said, "this is a twenty footer"!

I thought he was referring to the length of the car. But he corrected me. "No," he said. "I was referring to the fact that, at twenty feet, you might be fooled to think this was a nice vehicle." However, upon closer inspection he saw that the seats and door panels had been recovered with vinyl covers instead of the original expensive real leather. It was not up to the standards that one would expect for a professional restoration. In addition, the convertible top cover was not in accordance with new specs and was a cheap replacement. As he examined the sheet metal, he pointed to flaws and areas where his magnet would not adhere which seemed to indicate "bondo" under the paint instead of metal.

He explained that most of the seasoned professionals had been burned more than once and had to learn quickly how to avoid costly mistakes or they wouldn't survive in that business. If I were to buy a car at auction, I would employ a professional to avoid a "twenty footer" or pay the "twenty footer" value. So too, in practice, be careful of the "twenty footer" client.

I will try to describe them. They just fired their last attorney. They try to control the process and your strategy. They question your fees and demand you drop everything and treat their matter as if it is the most important case in your caseload. Many of them will come into your office with "bondo" underneath. It won't be detectable to the new practitioner. But the seasoned attorney will pick up on subtle cues that the new lawyer will never notice.

Try to find a mentor and do a "ride along" as often as you can. When you are just starting out your time may be well spent observing a professional in action. Many solo practitioners tell me that learning to distinguish the good clients from the bad clients is one of the hardest lessons they ever learned. They say 20 percent of your clients will create 80 percent of your greatest headaches. Learn to turn them away in the first instance. And if you find yourself entangled with someone who proves to be a "twenty footer," get rid of them consistent with the rules of professional responsibility as they costs you time, money, and emotional capital that is better spent on authentic and quality clients.

Chapter 55

In and Out: Avoid Bias When Assessing Clients' Communication

A True Story

About ten years ago my wife and I went to visit my father in California from Michigan where we resided. At that time, he was in his eighties and had been observed and diagnosed as one manifesting symptoms of dementia.

We decided to take him out to eat to get him out of the assisted living facility. So we asked him where he would like to go. He said he would like a good hamburger. We asked him if he had a favorite place to go. He told us that he liked, "in and out" burgers. At that point, my wife and I looked at each other knowingly so as to say, "that is so cute, he sees the traffic directional signs at a burger joint instructing vehicles where to enter and exit and he thinks that is the name of the franchise." We assumed at his age and with his mental frailty, that he mistook those signs for the name of the franchise. And rather than embarrass him, we decided to say nothing and pretend he was making sense. In the end, we took him to a local restaurant and enjoyed spending the rest of the day with him and thought nothing more of it.

Several days later while we were traveling in California, my wife said, "Stop the car!" I pulled the car over and asked what the matter was. She said, "Look behind us and across the street."

And there it was. The signage was unmistakable; there it was in big letters over the establishment: "In-N-Out Burger™." My father was correct and accurate in his description and we were the feebler of mind.

In practice, it is easy to misjudge individuals based on bias that we bring to the table. It is important to check ourselves when dealing with individuals who are reported to be suffering from dementia to evaluate them independently and objectively. Many of my clients suffer from hearing impairments that may affect their ability to understand or hear an inquiry properly. That hearing impairment leads to an answer that doesn't appear to make sense. A hearing impairment may mask itself as an inability to comprehend the meaning of a question.

We have often interviewed clients who have severe hearing loss and who consequently have been diagnosed with having dementia. During our assessment of some of those individuals, we provide a headset amplifier. It is remarkable the transformation that often takes place. From a person who is barely communicative, they turn into a "Chatty Kathy" and find that they were competent and had been misdiagnosed.

Similarly, a person who has suffered from a stroke can often experience cognitive deficiencies that resolve themselves fully or to a limited degree over time. This may mean that the affected individual's part of the brain that affects speech or the ability to say the name might be interpreted as a cognitive deficiency. Yet that person may be very capable of exercising good judgment or may regain that ability within a short period of time. Yet it is a steep slope for the patient to climb to overcome the prejudice many individuals experience once labeled as "incompetent."

Similar bias may be present when a husband and wife meet with you to engage in a discussion about their estate planning. It is not uncommon for spouses to cover for one another if one of them is experiencing the early stages of senility. As parents age, it becomes increasingly more difficult to overcome the prejudice that many individuals harbor concerning assumptions that their children may wish to take over and manage their affairs. As parents, you don't want your children to make decisions and hamper your freedom and flexibility. I often see children of senior parents intervene to "help" their parents. They tell the parents that they need to move to a safer environment like a condo. The parents have lived in the same location for forty years and have friends and systems established that give them predictability in their daily activities. Even if there is greater security in a different environment, that doesn't mean they are interested in change.

As a result, the parent becomes the "child" in the children's eyes and requires oversight. If one of the spouses sees their mate in decline, the first thing they do is cover for the spouse who is declining so that the kids don't get wind of the digression. When you meet those couples, you will see extreme resistance to independent interviews. Sometimes, it is because they really believe they possess the information that the attorney will need to know in concert with their spouse's interview. But on other occasions they will want to be present to cover for their spouse's erratic or deficient behavior. If you have a spouse experiencing the early stages of dementia in the room with her spouse, it will be difficult to get any answer from her other than a yes or no designed to endorse her spouse's decisions. We might attribute that behavior to the common delegation of powers over finances from one spouse to the other. The one who is more willing to pay the bills and take care of the finances is the designated financial manager in many marriages. But distinguishing delegation from declining mental acuity is quite a different matter.

Your assessment of your client's competence and ability to reason without assistance is critical as you engage in legal activities with your client. Make sure you separate your own prejudices or suspend your judgment until you have fully and fairly evaluated each of your clients in relation to the legal process involved. Document all of the evidence supporting your client's actions.

Make sure you do a critical and unbiased assessment. See what you can do to help your clients demonstrate their true abilities and you will be a better advocate.

Chapter 56

Some Final Words: The Dirty Dozen Tips for Solos

In 2003, which is an eternity away in terms of technology, I circulated a survey to over 2,800 solo practitioners in the state of Michigan in an attempt to determine factors that would predict success in solo practice. Facebook wasn't launched until 2004, and LinkedIn wasn't launched until 2003, payphones peaked in 1995, and have been made almost obsolete by 2011.

The survey was crafted with the help of analysts to derive scientifically valid data. It was also very long and tedious for the respondents to complete. It was over six pages long with almost twenty-five questions per page. At that time, SurveyMonkey had not matured as it was founded only in 1999. And I chose to use a paper format as my platform. What is surprising is that even though it was time-consuming to complete, and it required the time and effort to apply postage to return it, I still got 339 of those surveys returned. This tells me a lot about the hearts and souls of this profession. That that many busy souls would take the significant time and effort to share what they learned with others for no personal gain is a tribute to our profession.

In the end, I was unable to find factors that law students possessed that were predictive of success in solo practice later on. None of the factors I assessed stood out or proved to correlate with one another. But what I did get was a wealth of information shared by those respondents in the "Comments" section where I asked for their advice on what a new solo should know. With over 600 separate comments, I categorized them as best I could as dealing with various topics, like money management, niche practice, marketing, and so on. At the top of the list was money management, which was no surprise to me and should be of no surprise to any of you out there who have been in practice for any length of time.

The comments from the participants numbered in the hundreds and I took some time to review all of them before I embarked on my journey to help my law school graduates find success in solo practice. What follows is a sampling of some of those comments and they are representative of many of the comments handwritten with extra postage attached and sent to my office for my review. When you consider the time and effort each of those attorneys spent to make their ideas known, it is very impressive. It demonstrates what I have known all along—most solo practitioners are some of the most generous and thoughtful attorneys in practice today. If you want assistance or mentoring, go to a solo and seek it. Not all, but most understand the value of their time, but the key is that it is THEIRS TO GIVE. They are not throttled back or restricted by a partner or their concern to make partner.

I picked a baker's dozen:

1. Remember to live life and have fun.
2. Most opportunities don't come knocking; you have to be ready to make things happen.
3. Remember—every minute of the day contributes to your reputation.
4. Set realistic goals, but be flexible to change course if necessary.
5. Watch your cash flow—in other words, keep overhead and fixed costs low and always have cash reserves. (multiple responses)
6. Do not expect to become rich or even very comfortable. (I would dispute the comfortable part, but I am only the reporter.)
7. Expect a lack of collegiality.
8. Expect to work like hell.
9. In all retained cases, get the money up front, get the money up front, get the money up front, etc. (multiple responses)
10. Forget retirement.
11. Find specific areas of law and become an expert in those areas. (multiple responses)
12. Find a working spouse with benefits. (multiple responses)
13. The good news is that you can "tailor" your practice to do what you like to do and, in time, you will be able to regulate your life in accordance with your own desires, etc. (several like this)

I agree with many of these comments and disagree with some of them. For instance, "forget retirement" is true if you don't have a solid business plan and execute on it. The respondents could choose to remain anonymous, and many did. I suspect the person who wrote that comment was far along in his or her practice and without good planning found that to be true. However, part of any good business plan is to set aside reserves and a portion of your income as a matter of course. There will be times when it just isn't there, but there will be times when you feel that you can do no wrong and the cash flow is significant. The key is to balance that time out so that you understand that there will be peaks and valleys and to plan accordingly.

These are a few select comments. Most of the comments were focused on the business and management aspects of running a law office and some very profound. Overall, it was a mixed message about going solo or not going down that path. There were a few who said don't do it and just as many who were very encouraging. Some of the respondents made numerous suggestions and the sum of those with multiple comments, either good or bad gave me a pretty clear picture of whether they were making it or not. What I would say from the overall picture, is that you can be highly successful or fail miserably in this business. It isn't the profession or the style of practice that dictates the outcome; it is the person in charge.

As I was putting some finishing touches on this manuscript, a recent graduate stopped by to chat with me to find out how it was going and to congratulate me on receiving the Solo Trainer Award from the American Bar Association. During our conversation, I lamented the fact that as lawyers we do a very poor job of educating the public of the true value of legal counsel. In my opinion, there is plenty of work out there for attorneys and good paying work. Many attorneys in the field will dispute this; at least, the ones who are struggling will take that stand.

The reason so many new lawyers struggle is that they never understood that it is about reading the client to understand that client's needs and addressing them that will turn the tide and help them feel that they are getting value for their hard-earned money. There are some situations in which it doesn't matter how hard you work and how well you meet your client's objectives; they still feel pain when it comes time to pay you. Family law cases are like that. Rarely does one party leave the relationship feeling that the money spent on their divorce was a good "investment." Instead, you do what you can to minimize the pain and expense and help them through the trauma of divorce. One reason why I prefer estate planning is that the clients, even though they are facing their mortality, still feel that you have put in place a plan of action that needs to be addressed.

But every day, I see clients who have attempted to prepare their own legal documents and failed miserably. Some of their efforts have permanent and lasting negative consequences. Some of them can be rectified. If we did more to educate the public about the legal horror stories we see in our practices, I believe more nonlawyers would think twice about representing themselves or preparing their own documents.

I hope this book has given you the impetus to go out and research your options. If you do the work before you graduate to find out what the local Bar has to say about how they made it, or didn't, you will be better prepared to take advantage of their successes and avoid some of the mistakes that they have made along the way. That is the best education you will ever get, but you have to do the legwork to find your own way. Consider the alternative and see if those you visit have struggled without a plan or if those who are successful are working from a plan of action tailored to focus on a specialized area of law and taking full advantage of the tools that fit their needs. They are not taking on every new bit of technology, but moving forward with care and caution, but always moving forward. Keep looking outward and continue to innovate to stay on top of your game. If you do, you will find financial success, flexibility, some uncertainty, some success, and some failure. If you are not failing, you are not trying.

May you step outside your comfort zone.

He who is outside his door has the hardest part of his journey behind him.

Flemish Proverb

Good luck in your endeavors and may the wind be always at your back.

Tips and Tricks for Effective Interviews with Established Practitioners

Set Up—To Get a Busy Practitioner to Even Meet with You

Many attorneys will avoid meeting you at all costs. Largely because they have limited time to devote to a non business venture and many of them will see you as someone who is looking for a job—and THEY ARE NOT HIRING! Do not email them and expect a reply. Emails can be easily ignored, especially from someone you don't recognize. If you have contacts from past work with attorneys, draw upon them to assist you in exploring your options and obtain information to help you to find the right fit for your personality, experience, skills, and attributes. How do you get an interview without prior contacts?

1. Go to court and visit a judge. Introduce yourself and tell him/her that you plan to practice in their jurisdiction. Engage in small talk and ask the judge how they got where they are. Ask them to talk about herself

and you do 25 percent of the talking and let them do 75 percent of the talking. Use that rule of thumb when doing any interview. If the tables are turned, you will not be engaging. After you have completed your interview, ask the judge for the names of several attorneys in the area who are respected and competent attorneys. Ask for the names of some solo practitioners, not the large firm lawyers. The solos own their time, the large firm lawyers (unless they are partner) do not. The solos will be more generous with their time and they had to learn it all—the practice skills and the BUSINESS skills. This is what you want. SEND A THANK YOU CARD TO THE JUDGE THANKING HIM OR HER FOR HIS OR HER TIME (do not send an email) and you will be remembered in a good way.

Altenatively, visit a court clerk, not the judge's law clerk, but the clerk who administers the front counter and accepts documents for filing. When meeting with the clerk, use your judgement and do not try to engage in a conversation with the clerk during busy times of the day. When you meet and begin a conversation, pay attention to the body language and eye contact that you get from that person. If you feel that they are really attentive, ask them for their assistance in finding someone who you can interview who treats subordinates and others with respect and someone who has a good reputation in the area with the judges and other attorneys. The clerks often know more about attorneys and their reputations than some of the judges.

2. Now, contact the attorneys who the JUDGE RECOMMENDED or the CLERK RECOMMENDED and tell them that SO AND SO sent you to speak with them. They will not ignore the referral from a judge or a clerk!

3. A second method to get a referral from someone with the "horse-power" to get you in the door is to contact the local or state Bar officers and make the same inquiry in the same manner with them. Most of the active members of the Bar are reliable and connected resources. A referral from the President of the State Bar or Local Bar will be considered and probably acknowledged in the same manner as a judge.

4. When you contact the attorneys you want to interview, tell them who sent you. Do this by phone to the attorney or the attorney's staff member. Do not send an email. Emails are easy to delete.

5. When you first speak to that attorney MAKE IT CLEAR THAT YOU DO NOT WANT A JOB WITH THAT ATTORNEY AND THAT YOU ARE ONLY INVESTIGATING YOUR OPTIONS FOR PRACTICE AND YOU WANT TO SEE HOW THEY GOT WHERE THEY DID IN THIS PROFESSION.

6. When you get your appointment, DRESS BUSINESS CASUAL. If you dress like an interview, you will be perceived as conducting a job interview in disguise and that interview will be short. Reemphasize the fact that I have sent you out to investigate your options and to pick their brains—NOTHING MORE.

7. After your interview, send him or her a thank you card. You may as well get a packet of these and stamps from the stationery store as you will need them.

8. Before you meet with the attorney, order a box of business cards with your contact information and leave a card with everyone you meet. Make your card clean and simple. If you want to impress, pick a unique color but that is all. Be tasteful.

What Do You Ask When You Do Your Interview?

Write down key words to view as you do your interview (I will put them in bold type below), glance at your sheet to see if you covered everything, but do not break your eye contact any more than necessary. Be truly interested in the attorney as a person. Where did they come from, who inspired them, why law, do they have siblings, small talk . . . but essential to set the stage for them to open up to you. What do you ask about? Here are some suggestions:

What are they **doing well**?

What could they **do better**?

How did this **improve their bottom line**, or efficiency?

Is this something **you can adopt** from their practice?

What area or **areas of law** did they pursue initially?

Do they still practice that area of law? If not, why not?

How did they choose where they established their practice?

Who **mentored them**? How did they establish that relationship?

What are the **unique strengths** that they felt they brought to their practice?

What was the **greatest weakness** they had to overcome?

How did they decide **when to establish** their solo practice?

How did they **finance their practice**?

What were their **start-up expenses** and **first-year budget**?

How did they choose a computer?

How did they choose their software?

What kind of cloud or docket storage do they use?

What do they use to conduct legal research?

What kind of printer do they use?

Do they have a scanner?

Are they paperless?

How do they obtain malpractice insurance?

Do they have a brick and mortar office or sequestered environment or virtual practice?

What do they do for furnishings?

How do they advertise?

What is their budget for advertising?

What kind of phone system do they recommend?

How do they handle health Insurance?

How did they organize their practice? Sole proprietor, PLLC, Partner? Why?

What **social networking** do they use, if any?

What **web presence** do they have, if any?

What **professional organizations** do they participate in?

Finally, how do they distinguish themselves from other attorneys in their area? In their practice specialty?

Is it their ability to communicate?

Is it their personal connections?

How do they stay abreast of developments in the law and business in general to stay fresh and competitive?

Use this information to establish your own business plan as you go forward. If you decide to seek employment with someone else, keep that business plan in your back pocket and use that as a viable backup plan in the event you don't get the terms that you seek with that potential employer.

Good luck in your professional development.

Index

historical prejudice, 21–22
prejudice, 20
working with law firms, 19–20
disaster preparedness, 191–194
backup plans, 192
data and geographic redundancy, 192
implementation of backup plan, 192
location of data storage, 192
recovery from disaster and, 193
reviewing the backup system, 192
discounts, 164
divorce, 136–137, 145–146
document retrieval, 177–178
do-it-yourself lawyering, 165–166
dower, 136
Dragnet (television show), 40
driving and creativity, 41
drones, 70–71
Dropbox, 86, 184

E

earnings, 97–101
Easy Voice Recorder, 185
Eisenhower, Dwight, 57
Eisenhower planning technique, 49, 57
elitism, 21
emails, 193–194
emotional capital, 210–212
encryption, 85
enthusiasm, 50–51
Equine Law, 51
equine law, 148–152
ernietheattorney.net (blog), 194
essential tools, 81–89
computers, 83–84
data storage devices, 85–86
digital cloud storage, 86
malpractice insurance, 82–83
office space, 88–89
practice management software, 87–88
printers, 87
scanners, 84–85
smart phones, 88

estate planning
clients with dementia and, 228
fees, 142–143
microniche in, 172–173
niche practice, 145
pets and, 138–139
specialization in, 150–151
trust protector, 139
Evernote, 184
exams, 65
execution of documents, 161–162
exercise, 41
expenses, management of, 93–94

F

Facebook, 158, 231
family law practitioners, 136, 145
Fastcase, 187–190
fearlessness in solo practice, 37–40
fear of failure, 23
fear of success, 23–25
Federal Aviation Administration
(FAA), 71
Ferstman, Julie, 50–51
financial collapse of 2005, 39
financial dependency, 39
first job
business plan, 107–108
finding/making your, 107–110
going to court, 108–109
going where attorneys gather, 109–110
first year in law school
defining your brand, 124–126
determining geographic areas of interest, 115
finding influencers, 125–126
going to court to mix and mingle, 123–124
minimizing student debt, 115–116
understanding types of practice, 115
fiverr®, 179–180
flash drives, 85, 192
Foonberg, Jay, 4, 148